Fountaindale
Public Library District

D1174313

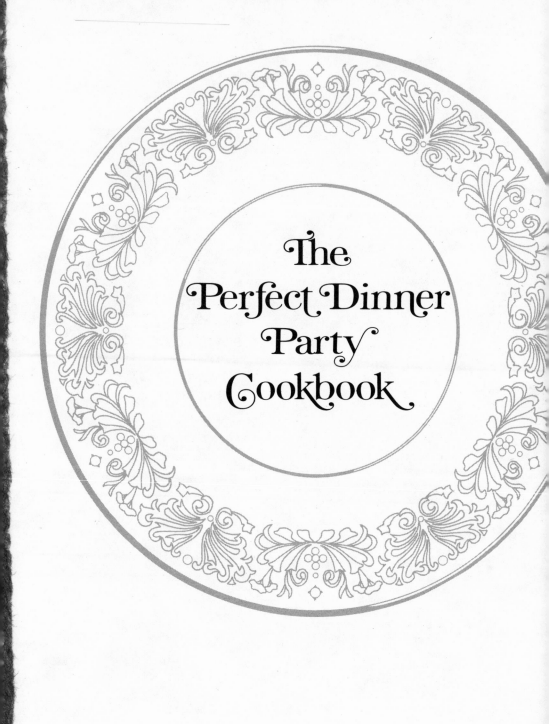

The Perfect Dinner Party Cookbook

DAVID McKAY
COMPANY,
INC.
NEW YORK

The Perfect Dinner Party Cookbook

—

CEIL DYER

BY THE SAME AUTHOR:

Sweet Taste of Success: A Book of Desserts

The Freezer Cookbook

Hamburgers Plain and Fancy

The Plan Ahead Cookbook

The Quick and Easy Electric Skillet Cookbook

The Quick Gourmet Cookbook

The Newport Cookbook

All Around the Town (in collaboration with Roz Cole)

⊙

The Perfect Dinner Party Cookbook
Copyright © 1974 by Ceil Dyer

Library of Congress Catalog Card Number: 73-91117
ISBN 0-679-50454-0
Manufactured in the United States of America
Designed by The Etheredges

⊙

To Lady Tootsie Williams
who enjoyed the dinner parties
most of all

The author wishes to thank
the Towle Silver Company
for the use of their beautiful flatware
and the British Allied Potters
for the use of their distinguished
Royal Crown Derby and
Minton china.
They created memorable settings.

Contents

Introduction

"No man ever committed suicide after a good dinner." Who could? A good dinner among good friends is one of life's most civilized pleasures. The day's problems fade and tomorrow is surely going to be much better.

A good dinner party, even a great dinner party, need not be difficult to prepare or to serve in a leisurely, graceful way. Though help has largely vanished from the kitchen and the dinning room, a simpler style of eating has replaced the seven-course affairs of our grandmothers—and all to the good. Anyone who has ever read Booth Tarkington's unforgettable *Alice Adams* knows that the overelaborate menus and the fussily decorated table are the twin evils of pleasurable dining. However, simplicity does not mean starkness. A good dinner party is, above all, a festive occasion: marvelous food; a menu well suited to the mood and the season; the atmosphere, gay, warm and relaxed; and the setting glowing with color, with flowers, candles, and that indefinable something called ambience.

WHY GIVE A DINNER PARTY?

The art of giving a great dinner party can stand you in good stead. There is no better way to make new circles of friends or renew old ones. For the single woman, dinner parties are the nicest way to get to know that interesting new man. For the bachelor they are an intriguing way to "pay back." For the older woman, they're marvelous opportunities to broaden her social life. For the stranger, they are a perfect way to "break in." And for a couple, they are the golden road to a warm circle of friends of all ages, a place in the community—and they are also the most effective way for a wife to help her husband succeed in business with just a little trying.

The best reason for giving dinner parties, however, is for pure and simple enjoyment. Far more enjoyable than the cocktail party, and much more personal, dinner parties offer you the opportunity to share with your friends your best efforts—food, flowers, and wine that you have chosen with taste, imagination, and a touch of wit.

I hope you feel about parties as I do. I *like* to give them. If I had my way, life would be one party after another from New Year's Day to New Year's Eve.

After giving so many parties for so many people over the years, I naturally have some definite ideas about them. First, never give a party you can't afford and never invite anyone you don't really like. In either case you will be ill at ease, and no matter how grand the food, how beautiful the table, your guests will sense and reflect your mood.

I want my parties to be festive and gay, and I want the food to be superb. What I aim for is a relaxed, happy atmosphere with everyone at their best—and I want to be at my best too.

How is it possible to achieve these results? It took me a number of years to find all the answers, and there are still a few that elude me at times, but the key word is planning.

I have divided this book into six sections, each devoted to a different type of party and how to go about giving it, but planning and doing ahead is the way to success for any one of them.

PARTY PLANNING

Ordinarily I like to set a date that will allow everybody two to three weeks' advance notice. After deciding on the kind of party I'm going to give and how many people I'm going to invite, I select the menu, then engage whatever help I will need and reserve any special equipment I will want to rent. After this, never before (or I'm in trouble if either help or equipment is not available), I issue invitations—by telephone if it's to be a small, intimate gathering or by handwritten notes if it's to be a large, festive occasion or a formal dinner.

PARTY EQUIPMENT

The next step is a check list of things I will need—cooking equipment, china, flatware, linens, glasses and serving dishes, etc.—to make sure I have the quantity and the style for the type of party I am going to give. Then I buy, make, or borrow what's not on hand.

PARTY STRATEGY

About one week before the party I make a grocery list, order special foods that will take time to be delivered, and shop for staple groceries. I check my bar and stock the necessary liquor and any special wine I am going to serve with the meal. At this point I also order flowers—to make sure I'll get what I want in colors that will coordinate with my other decorations—and I order extra ice, both to be delivered early on the day of the party.

THREE OR FOUR DAYS AHEAD

I decide on seating arrangements and, if I am going to use them, write place cards. If I am unsure of how the final production may turn out, I stage a dress rehearsal of my table settings and test out on my family any part of the menu that I have not made before. I also prepare any frozen dessert or such other food that can be made this far ahead.

THE DAY BEFORE

I have my hair done. I shop for groceries. Then I cook that food which can be prepared in advance. I arrange the house for the event and, if it's a large party, set up the extra tables and special decorations.

ON THE BIG DAY

As early as possible I prepare all food that was not made the day before. I then set my table or tables, arrange the flowers, set up the bar, and check the powder room and hall closet to make sure they are equipped and in order.

NOW ON TO THE PARTY ITSELF

About two hours before guests are due to arrive, I neat up the kitchen, fill up the dishwasher with used cooking equipment, and put out serving pieces. I remove cooked food from the refrigerator and bring it to room temperature so that it will be easier to reheat. I then prepare any food that could not be made earlier. If I'm going to have outside help serve the meal, they will arrive about this time and I brief them on how I want the details handled. After this, I take a leisurely bath and get dressed. Back downstairs, I finish last-minute cooking, fill up the ice bucket, and—I'm on schedule. My guests arrive and after they have been served one drink I return to the kitchen for the last minute inspection and preparation. The party is well under way. We're going to have a wonderful time.

Seated Dinner Parties

⊙

YOUR GUESTS

The choice of guests should be your first consideration for a seated dinner. Good food is important, of course, and so is a festive table, but do start with the right mix of people—people who will truly enjoy being together. At a large buffet your guests can move from group to group, but at a seated dinner they are held together around one table for a good part of the evening. A happy maximum is eight guests, but four or six is even nicer. Beyond eight the serving becomes more complicated, and the ambience of a cozy group is lost. That is not to say you can't have twelve, sixteen, twenty, or more guests for dinner successfully, but unless you have ample help they are best served at a buffet. For this reason all of the recipes in this section are planned for eight servings.

If you plan on serving six or more, place cards are a good idea. They help avoid confusion and delay in seating and let you place your guests where you think they will contribute their best to the party. To keep everyone happy and relaxed and the conversation flowing, try to picture your guests together. Who will enjoy talking to whom? Try to alternate talkers and listeners. One witty conversationalist is lost next to another, and two listeners listening side by side can hardly add to the festivities. It is true that the way you set your table and serve can help make the meal go smoothly, but if anyone is stuck with an incompatible neighbor, he or she will find the evening a bore no matter how great the food.

INVITATIONS

Once you have decided *who* to ask, your next decision will be *when*. The best way to eliminate the necessity of a change in your original blend of guests is to telephone rather than write your invitations and start with tentative dates. Ask your first guests, "Are you free Friday or Saturday night?" If both evenings are open, you can go on to explain that you want them to get together with "the Smiths," and you will check back as soon as you find which evening the latter are free.

EQUIPMENT

Having set the date, you can begin to map out the evening. Start by deciding on a menu, then think out how you will serve each item from cocktails to after dinner coffee. First check to see if you have necessary equipment both to cook and serve the meal. If you have never prepared a dish that you plan to serve, try it out on your family a few nights before the party; and if you are uncertain as to how the table will look, have a "dress rehearsal" —set it a day ahead so that you will have ample time to buy, borrow or rent any missing articles. See what silver needs polishing and check the lighting.

LIGHTING

Absolutely nothing dampens a party mood so decidedly as glaring, unflattering lights. Try for a soft but not too dim effect. Candles definitely, but if your room is fairly large you may also need a couple of well-placed lamps (try pink-tinted bulbs in them.) Never use an overhead chandelier; it makes everyone look deadly.

PARTY STRATEGY

Try to think of the evening as a whole, starting where your guests arrive. Does the hall closet contain enough sturdy hangers for heavy coats? Is it clean and attractive? Now your living room. Are there enough chairs? Will the seating arrangement divide the party into isolated groups or will it work to bring people together? If people are going to help themselves to drinks, can you set up your bar where it is easy to get to? (I use a small pantry that divides my living room from the kitchen, which makes it easy to refill the ice bucket, but any convenient spot will do—a corner in the living room, the entry hall if it's large enough, or the terrace if weather permits.)

STOCKING THE BAR

While you are thinking about drinks and their serving, it's a good time to order supplies. If you know your guests' preferences, this is easy. If not, simply stock your bar with the basics: Scotch, bourbon, vodka, gin, and blended whiskey. Don't forget to order ice, if your refrigerator can't handle the crowd, as well as soda. And don't forget tomato juice and grapefruit juice for nondrinkers and sherry or an aperitif for those who like their drinks light.

HORS D'OEUVRES

This brings you to hors d'oeuvres. Remember that whatever you serve must complement the meal to come. Unless there is a cook in the kitchen, eliminate anything that must be served hot from the oven and forget too about fussy canapes that become soggy and limp if kept waiting. Actually, the simpler the choice the better.

I usually serve crisp cheese straws, smoked salmon rolled up and speared with cocktail picks, and a variety of raw vegetables surrounding a piquant dip. I pass the hors d'oeuvres once, then place them around the room where people can help themselves. Other easy choices are jumbo pickled cocktail onions, ripe olives, thin pretzel sticks, paté, or cold boiled shrimp. The point is to serve a variety but at the same time keep it light and on the sparse side or appetites will be spoiled for the meal to come.

HIRING EXTRA HELP

If your budget is limited or if help is not available, it takes very little extra effort to handle the evening alone. Service can be more formal, however, if you have one person to help. Whenever possible I hire someone to serve the meal, then stay to clean up.

If you don't have a good, reliable part-time helper who is used to your ways and willing to work in the evening, club personnel are often happy to earn extra money on their night off. Other good sources for well-trained help are hotel dining rooms (ask the maître d'), one of your town's better restaurants, and of course your own party-giving friends. And don't overlook a local college where you can often find willing if not trained students to serve and clean up—if you show them how.

With any help you hire, always discuss how they want to be paid and establish the rate. They may want payment in cash and you will need to have it on hand. Make sure they know how to get to your house or apartment, and also find out if they have uniforms.

You may have to supply these, which is reasonable if you are going to use the same person again, but if you are not sure about a repeat appearance, try to rent or borrow them.

Whether you plan to do it all yourself or hire someone to help, your bar should be set up, the table set, and all food cooked before your guests arrive. I usually manage to do this in time to fix myself a relaxing drink and sit down and drink it before the doorbell begins to ring.

When you aren't planning to have help, the meal can be served in either of two ways.

SERVICE WITHOUT HELP

At an informal party the first course is on the table when guests are seated. When it is finished you can clear away, alone or with the help of one person—but never more than one or confusion will reign. Then guests help themselves to the main course which has been previously arranged on the sideboard or on a wall table—buffet style. Again you will clear away and everyone helps himself to dessert from a second smaller buffet table —or you may wish to serve the dessert from a previously arranged tray.

For a service that is a bit more formal, you should have a small table with a lower shelf—or, still better, one of those handy two-shelf rolling serving carts. Your dining table should be completely set with dessert fork and spoon placed horizontally directly above the service plate.

Just before dinner is announced, place the prepared salad plates on the table to the left of the forks. Then set up the main course on a covered platter and place it on the top shelf of your serving table or cart along with the main-course plates, serving spoon and fork. If you are going to have a cheese course, place the cheese and plates on the second shelf, and put the dessert on dessert plates on the sideboard. Arrange the first course on the table, fill the wine glasses, and dinner is served.

When the first course is completed you can take the used plates to the kitchen while your husband (if you have one—if not, any man you appoint as host for the evening) places the main-course platter in front of him, serves the plates, and passes them to each guest. After the main course is finished, the used plates are placed on the second shelf of the serving table or cart and the cheese plates are placed on the table. At the conclusion of the cheese course, remove the cheese plates and salad plates as well as salt and pepper shakers to the serving table or cart.

Guests can now help themselves to dessert or sip a last bit of wine as you serve it.

Coffee is served in the living room at the conclusion of either type meal.

For either service the wine is placed near the host—red wine on the table in a wine basket, white wine in an ice bucket—and he is responsible for refilling the glasses.

WITH HELP

When you hire someone for the first time to serve a meal, remember he or she will be unfamiliar with your household, your menu, and your equipment, so ask them to come early enough to allow time to explain what, when, why, and how you want everything done.

All food should be cooked and the table set before your helper arrives. Don't expect anyone new to your kitchen to find necessary china and silver. Have it ready. Service for each course should be set out on the kitchen counter—in fact, prepare everything possible beforehand, from appetizer platter to coffee tray, so that your server can concentrate on serving the meal beautifully while you relax and enjoy your guests.

For an example of how things should go and what your helper can do, let's take our first menu. As I said, whoever you hire should be on hand for a thorough briefing before the party begins. Then, after you have greeted your guests and seen that they have cocktails in the living room, you can slip back to the kitchen and place the room-temperature coquilles in a preheated oven. The duck has been previously carved and is waiting in a warming oven ready to be placed on a nearby serving platter along with the accompaniments. If you have an electric hot tray, the platter may be already arranged and placed on it. If not, tell your server exactly how to arrange it. The currant jelly should be ready in a crystal or silver bowl on its own plate with a serving spoon. The salad is already on plates in the refrigerator, and the cheese is coming to room temperature on its serving plate with a knife. Crackers are in a napkin-lined basket. The afterdinner coffee, made in a glass or earthenware pot, is standing in a pan of barely simmering water and is ready to be poured into a heated serving pot.

Cheese plates are on a side table in the dining room as is dessert. Finally, the champagne, which has been opened, is cooling in an ice bucket near the host's chair.

The coquilles are placed on the table and the wine glasses filled before dinner is announced. When you have finished the first course, the plates as well as the service plates are removed, two at a time, and returned to the kitchen where the server picks up two of the entrée plates and sets them in front of the guests whose places have been cleared. The process is then repeated until the entire table is cleared. The server then passes the entrée platter and follows with the currant jelly. The same procedure is followed for the salad which in this case is served as a separate course as it is accompanied by cheese. After the salad course, dessert is served in the same manner.

Incidentally, it's a good idea to have your server "neat up" the living room—empty ash trays and take cocktail glasses to the kitchen—after dessert is served. Then the only task left for the helper before cleaning up is to fill the coffeepot and bring the coffee service to the living room.

TABLE DECORATIONS

Now that the "how to" is established and cooking strategy mapped out, you can turn to the pleasant task of decorating your party table. A lot depends on the dishes you plan to use but there are inexpensive ways to add to your present service plates that make the difference between dreary dull and party perfection.

For example, clear glass first-course plates can be bought for very little at most variety stores—they don't have to be top quality —and they look very attractive over almost any service plate, patterned or plain. They can also double as salad or dessert plates. Pretty, too, for salads are those inexpensive green pottery leaf plates. For dessert service, why not try something really different? Serve ice cream or fruit desserts in big globe-shaped wine glasses, or use small lacquer trays (available in Japanese shops) for cake service.

Soups, too, can be presented with a flair. Hollow out a small leafy cabbage to hold a glass bowl of chilled soup for each guest, or serve soups in individual covered tureens.

As for the table itself, forget about tablecloths for any but the most formal dinners, which are not our concern here. Instead, for a beautifully serene effect, start with a bare polished table or

use place mats. Good-looking mat and napkin sets are often quite
inexpensive, but if you like to sew it's even more fun to make your
own. Here is where you can let your imagination go as far as you
like. Quite often, drapery and slipcover fabrics make wonderful
table linens and the colors are superb. Usually such materials are
48 inches or 50 inches wide so they are economical too. Just make
sure the fabric is washable—and as with every other aspect of your
party, do give yourself ample time for the making.

Here are a few combinations that work well:

SPRING
MATS: *white organdy*
NAPKINS: *parrot green*
SERVICE PLATES: *flower-sprigged china*
FIRST-COURSE PLATES: *glass*
WINE GLASSES: *delicate crystal*
DESSERT SERVICE: *green leaf plates*
CENTERPIECE: *pink tulips in a crystal or silver bowl*

SUMMER
MATS: *brown suede cloth*
NAPKINS: *pale beige cotton*
SERVICE PLATES: *brown pottery*
FIRST-COURSE PLATES: *wood (if soup is served, use hollowed-out
    cabbage on wood plate)*
WINE GLASSES: *heavy crystal*
DESSERT SERVICE: *small shallow baskets holding brown pottery
    plates*
CENTERPIECE: *weathered country basket of mixed garden flowers or
    seasonal vegetables*

FALL
MATS: *blue and white checked gingham*
NAPKINS: *bright red*
SERVICE PLATES: *heavy white ironstone*
FIRST-COURSE PLATES: *pewter*
WINE GLASSES: *heavy crystal*
DESSERT SERVICE: *shallow basket with white ironstone plates*
CENTERPIECE: *basket of highly polished apples*

WINTER
MATS: *white linen*
NAPKINS: *deep violet-blue*
SERVICE PLATES: *white china*
FIRST-COURSE PLATES: *glass*
WINE GLASSES: *delicate crystal*
DESSERT SERVICE: *glass*
CENTERPIECE: *small pots of violets*

SPECIAL OCCASIONS

EASTER
MATS: *pale pink*
NAPKINS: *pale green*
SERVICE PLATES: *white china*
FIRST-COURSE PLATES: *green leaf plates*
WINE GLASSES: *delicate crystal*
DESSERT SERVICE: *glass*
CENTERPIECE: *six small pots of assorted spring bulbs, hyacinths, crocuses, daffodils, tulips, etc., each pot tied with a bow of pastel ribbon* NOT *matching the flowers.*

FOURTH OF JULY
MATS: *bright blue*
NAPKINS: *red bandanas*
SERVICE PLATES: *heavy white ironstone*
FIRST-COURSE PLATES: *wood*
WINE GLASSES: *heavy crystal*
DESSERT SERVICE: *deep-blue bowls on white ironstone plates*
CENTERPIECE: *child's drum filled with red zinnias*

THANKSGIVING
MATS: *yellow linen*
NAPKINS: *deep brown*
SERVICE PLATES: *white ironstone*
FIRST-COURSE PLATES: *wood*
WINE GLASSES: *heavy crystal*
DESSERT SERVICE: *pewter or wood*
CENTERPIECE: *weathered basket of sheaves of corn and dried grasses*

CHRISTMAS
MATS: *shocking pink*
NAPKINS: *shocking pink*
SERVICE PLATES: *white china*
FIRST-COURSE PLATES: *glass*
WINE GLASSES: *delicate crystal*
DESSERT SERVICE: *glass*
CENTERPIECE: *bare branches hung with small pink Christmas balls*

AFTER DINNER

At our house at the end of the meal we return to the living room for coffee. There are two reasons. First, people can move around, mingle, and change conversational partners; second, if I have help they can clear the table, finish cleaning up, and go home —or I can serve coffee, then slip away without being missed to clear the table quickly, get a load of dishes in the dishwasher, put away leftover food, and generally neat up a bit.

What happens after dinner? If I know my guests and they know one another, it's usually just talk and more talk with more coffee and perhaps a cognac, but here are a few things I've done when I was not sure that people would entertain themselves.

When I had an apartment in New York I hired a palmist, a wonderfully witty woman who knew how to perform before a crowd. She told each person's fortune, the past and future, all very tactful, of course, while the rest of us stood around and listened. Great fun!

In Charleston, for my northern visitors, I hired a group of Gospel singers. They sang on my terrace. It was a beautiful spring night and the garden was flooded with moonlight—we all thought it very romantic.

At other parties I have rented a movie projector and some marvelous 1920 movies—Laurel and Hardy, Chaplin, Mary Pickford. If you live in a large city, consult the yellow pages of your telephone book for this service. I also once organized a mini square dance because I knew a charming man who could do the "calling." Another time I hired a carriage and took all my guests for a ride after dinner. But for the most part I have relied on really good food, soft lights, and a pretty room. I found that was all I needed to make my small seated dinner parties a success, and I think you will too.

⊙

SEATED DINNER #1
(SERVES EIGHT)

Coquilles of Crabmeat and Shrimp in Sherry Cream Sauce

Crisp Roast Duck

Fried Hominy Grits

Currant Jelly

Bibb Lettuce and Watercress Salad

Camembert or Brie Cheese

Unsalted Crackers

Glazed Baked Apples with Brandied Hard Sauce

Coffee

WINE: *Dry California Champagne*

⊙

COQUILLES OF CRABMEAT AND SHRIMP IN SHERRY CREAM SAUCE

6 tablespoons butter
6 tablespoons flour
1 cup milk
¼ cup sherry
1 egg yolk
1 cup heavy cream
Salt to taste
1 pound crabmeat
1 pound shrimp, cooked, peeled, and deveined
1 cup fine dry bread crumbs
4 tablespoons melted butter

Preheat oven to 350° F.

Melt the butter in a saucepan over low heat. Add flour and stir to a smooth paste. Cook for 1 or 2 minutes, stirring occasionally. Add milk gradually, stirring to blend. Cook over low heat until sauce begins to thicken. Add sherry and blend.

Beat the egg yolk in a small dish, spoon in 2 tablespoons of the hot sauce, and mix well. Pour the egg mixture into the sauce, stirring constantly. Add cream and salt and continue to cook over very low heat until sauce is thick.

Remove sauce from heat. Add crabmeat and shrimp. Pile mixture into coquilles (scallop shells). Sprinkle coquilles with bread crumbs and pour a little melted butter over each.

NOTE: At this point coquilles may be refrigerated until ready to heat. In this case they should be allowed to come to room temperature (about 20 minutes) before baking.

Bake about 10 to 15 minutes or until lightly browned.

⊙

CRISP ROAST DUCK

2 four- to five-pound Long Island ducklings
Salt
Lemon juice
1 seedless orange, cut in half
1 apple, cut into 4 wedges
1 small onion, peeled and cut in half
1 cup sauterne
½ cup brandy
8 broiled orange slices

If using frozen ducklings, defrost completely and bring to room temperature.

Preheat oven to 375° F.

Trim off loose fat and rub ducks with lemon juice and salt. In the cavity of each bird place ½ orange, 2 apple wedges, and ½ onion.

Place birds, breast side up, in roasting pan in preheated oven and roast for 20 minutes. Turn breast side down and roast for an additional 20 minutes. Remove roasting pan from oven. Pour off all grease, then return to oven. Reduce temperature to 350° F. and roast the ducks for 1 hour, basting frequently with the sauterne.

Remove ducks and allow them to cool slightly, then cover

and refrigerate until cold or until about 1 hour before serving. Strain the pan juices into a nonmetal storage bowl. Refrigerate until all the fat rises to the surface and congeals. Remove and discard fat. Refrigerate, covered, until ready to use.

TO REHEAT: Preheat oven to 375° F. Remove ducks from refrigerator and let stand at room temperature for 30 minutes. In a small saucepan, reheat pan juices. Place ducks in preheated oven for 30 minutes, basting frequently with warm pan juices.

TO SERVE: Cut ducks into serving pieces (discarding fruit stuffing). Place on serving platter and surround with broiled orange slices. Heat brandy over low flame, ignite, and pour over ducks and oranges. Bring flaming to the table.
Lovely.

○

FRIED HOMINY GRITS

4 cups water
1 cup grits
1 teaspoon salt
2 eggs
2 tablespoons water
1 cup cornmeal
2 cups salad oil

Bring the 4 cups of water to a boil, add grits and salt slowly, stirring rapidly to avoid lumping. Lower heat and cook slowly for 10 to 15 minutes, stirring occasionally until grits are thick and smooth but not stiff. Cool until grits are lukewarm. Butter the inside of two tall glasses, such as iced tea glasses, and pour the warm grits into the glasses. Chill until firm and quite cold. Remove grits from glasses by running a knife around the inside of the glass or by standing the glasses in warm, *not hot,* water for a moment or two. The grits will slide out in neat rolls. Cut the rolls into ½-inch slices. There should be 16 to 18 slices. Beat the eggs with the 2 tablespoons of water and place the cornmeal on a large flat surface such as a baking sheet. Dip the rounds first into the egg, then into the cornmeal; repeat the process a second time. Place

completed rounds on the baking sheet and refrigerate for at least
1 hour.

About an hour before serving, heat 1 cup of the salad oil in
a large, heavy skillet until a light haze forms and fry the rounds a
few at a time, turning once to brown evenly. Add additional oil
as needed. Drain the rounds on paper towels and keep hot in a
warm oven (about 250° F.) until ready to serve. They may be prepared as much as an hour ahead.

⊙

GLAZED BAKED APPLES
WITH BRANDIED HARD SAUCE

BAKED APPLES
8 large McIntosh or Rome Beauty apples
½ cup extra-fine granulated sugar
½ tablespoon lemon rind
8 teaspoons butter, at room temperature

Preheat oven to 375° F.

Wash apples and scoop out cores, leaving ½ inch of pulp at
the bottom. Combine sugar, butter, and rind.

Fill centers with mixture. Cover and bake 20 to 25 minutes or
until barely tender but not soft. Transfer apples to a deep skillet
and pour Glaze (*recipe below*) over them. Cook over low heat,
constantly basting with glaze until apples are shiny and glaze has
thickened. Remove to serving plates and cool to room temperature
before serving with Brandied Hard Sauce (*recipe below*).

GLAZE
1 cup orange juice
½ cup water
3 cups extra-fine granulated sugar
1 tablespoon butter
1 teaspoon grated orange rind
2 tablespoons Grand Marnier or Cointreau liqueur

Combine orange juice, water, sugar, and orange rind in a
small saucepan. Bring mixture to a boil. Lower heat and cook

until it forms large, heavy drops from the side of the spoon. Add brandy. Use immediately. If glaze becomes too firm, add a teaspoon or so of boiling water.

BRANDIED HARD SAUCE
5 tablespoons butter
1½ cups powdered sugar
3 tablespoons cognac or brandy
½ teaspoon grated lemon rind
2 tablespoons finely slivered toasted almonds

With butter at room temperature, cream until fluffy; add sugar and cream mixture until very light and smooth. Blend in cognac, lemon rind, and almonds. Chill well before serving. If desired, the sauce may be spread in a flat shallow pan before chilling and cut into small fancy shapes.

⊙

SEATED DINNER #2
(SERVES EIGHT)

Melon Slices with Anchovies and Peppers

Roast Loin of Pork with Prunes

Puree of Kidney Beans Basque Style

Spinach Salad

Strawberry Angel Grand Marnier

Coffee

WINE: *Bordeaux St. Julien*
ALTERNATE: *California Pinot Chardonnay*

An especially easy dinner, even for the novice cook. Everything may be prepared ahead and safely stand ready to serve for at least an hour after reheating.

⊙

MELON SLICES
WITH ANCHOVIES AND PEPPERS

An easy and eye-catching appetizer that is a perfect start for a somewhat substantial meal.

2 medium-size green peppers
4 tablespoons salad oil
1 teaspoon sugar
2 tablespoons lemon juice
1 teaspoon salt
1 teaspoon pepper
2 honeydew melons
16 anchovy fillets

Core the green peppers, removing all white membrane, and cut them into julienne strips. Heat 1 tablespoon of the oil in a small saucepan and sauté the strips until slightly soft.

Combine remaining oil, sugar, lemon juice, salt, and pepper in a small nonmetal bowl and blend well. Add pepper strips to mixture and refrigerate for several hours or overnight. Cut melons in half, peel, and cut again into half-moon slices. Arrange overlapping slices on plates, placing two anchovies on each serving. Add pepper strips and 1 or 2 teaspoons of dressing immediately before serving.

⊙

ROAST LOIN OF PORK
WITH PRUNES

This is a subtle and marvelous combination of flavors, the crisp pork and slightly sweet prunes complementing each other perfectly. And it is such an attractive dish!

> *1 two and one-half- to three-pound loin of pork, boned*
>   *(weight after boning)*
> *16 to 18 dried prunes, pitted and cooked*
> *¼ cup sugar*
> *2 tablespoons flour*
> *1 teaspoon salt*
> *1 teaspoon freshly ground black pepper*
> *1 teaspoon dried thyme*
> *1 teaspoon dried rosemary*
> *¾ cup dry white wine*

Preheat oven to 500° F.

Bring meat to room temperature.

Flatten the meat slightly with a wooden mallet. Place a row of cooked prunes down the center and roll up. Tie securely with butcher's string. Combine the flour, salt, pepper, and herbs and rub into the surface of the meat.

Place the pork in a shallow roasting pan, *not* on a rack, in the preheated oven and cook 5 to 10 minutes, then immediately lower heat to 300° F. and continue to cook for at least 30 minutes to the pound or until a meat thermometer inserted in the thickest part of the meat registers 190° F. Remove from oven. Pour off accumulated fat.

Heat the wine to just boiling and pour over hot meat. Baste continuously for 5 or 10 minutes, then allow the roast to stand for 20 to 30 minutes before carving.

COOKED PRUNES

Place prunes in a small saucepan and cover with cold water. Let soak for 2 or 3 hours. Add ¼ cup sugar and cook over medium heat until barely tender. Drain well.

⊙

PUREE OF KIDNEY BEANS
BASQUE STYLE

This is the French version of Mexican refried beans. The wine adds a sophisticated flavor. It's an excellent accompaniment to roast or broiled meat and a nice substitute for the usual potatoes or rice.

1 pound kidney beans
½ teaspoon salt
2 cups dry red wine
1 clove garlic, peeled
¼ pound salt pork
2 tablespoons flour
1 tablespoon butter, at room temperature
Salt and pepper to taste

Wash beans and place them in a large nonmetal bowl. Cover by at least 1 inch with cold water. Let soak 8 hours or overnight.

Place beans and soaking water in a large pot. Add additional water if needed to again cover by 1 inch. Cook over low heat until tender, about 2 hours. Add salt during the last 30 minutes of cooking. Drain beans, reserving liquid, and puree by forcing through a sieve.

Place wine and garlic in a small saucepan and cook over low heat until reduced by half. Remove and discard garlic.

Cut salt pork into small dices. Cover with water in a small pan and bring to boil. Lower heat and let simmer for 5 minutes. Drain and pat thoroughly dry.

Place diced, blanched pork in a large, heavy skillet and cook, stirring often, until all fat is rendered and pork cubes are crisp. Remove them with a slotted spoon to paper toweling to drain. Set aside.

Pour all but 1 tablespoon of the rendered fat from the skillet. Add the flour and cook, stirring mixture over low heat until smooth. Add wine and continue to stir until mixture thickens. Stir in the pureed beans, butter, and sufficient reserved bean liquid to give the consistency of mashed potatoes. Season with salt and pepper to taste. Sprinkle reserved crisp salt pork cubes over surface immediately before serving.

NOTE: If desired, this dish may be made ahead. Refrigerate, covered.

TO REHEAT: Add a little reserved bean liquid and stir over low heat until steamy.

○

SPINACH SALAD

8 slices bacon
2 pounds baby leaf spinach
½ cup salad oil
½ cup orange juice
2 tablespoons lemon juice
¼ tablespoon dry mustard
1 teaspoon sugar
¼ teaspoon salt
Sprinkling of freshly ground black pepper
1 tart apple, peeled, cored, and chopped

Broil or fry bacon until crisp and dry. Drain on paper toweling. Crumble and set aside.

Wash spinach, leaf by leaf, under cold running water. Tear large leaves into bite-size pieces. Blot dry with paper toweling.

To prepare dressing, combine oil, orange juice, lemon juice, mustard, sugar, and salt and pepper. Beat with a wire whisk until blended and frothy.

Place spinach in a large salad bowl. Add crumbled bacon and chopped apple. Toss well so that each spinach leaf is coated with dressing.

NOTE: Bacon, spinach, and dressing may all be prepared ahead. Wrap washed spinach loosely in wet paper toweling. Refrigerate until time to assemble salad. Toss chopped apple with lemon juice to prevent discoloration. Store in plastic bag in refrigerator.

Salad may stand at room temperature for as long as 30 minutes before serving. Longer than that and the spinach will become limp. Toss again just before serving.

⊙

STRAWBERRY ANGEL GRAND MARNIER

⅔ *cup coconut flakes*
⅓ *cup confectioners sugar*
¼ *teaspoon cream of tartar*
Dash of salt
2 *egg whites*
⅔ *cup granulated sugar*
1 *quart strawberries*
½ *cup Grand Marnier liqueur*
1 *cup heavy cream*

Preheat oven to 325° F.

Combine coconut flakes and confectioners sugar. Blend and set aside.

Sprinkle cream of tartar and salt over egg whites in a large bowl and beat until foamy. Add granulated sugar, 1 tablespoon at a time, beating well after each addition. Continue beating until mixture will stand in stiff peaks. Fold in the coconut.

Spread mixture on the bottom and sides of a lightly greased 9-inch pie pan. Bake in preheated (325° F.) oven for 30 minutes or until meringue feels dry and firm. Cool.

Hull and wash strawberries. Slice large berries, leaving small berries whole. Place in a bowl and add the Grand Marnier. Cover and let stand 1 hour or longer.

When ready to serve, drain strawberries, reserving liqueur. Whip cream until stiff, fold in strawberries, and fill meringue with mixture. Pour reserved liqueur over surface and serve at once.

○

SEATED DINNER #3
(SERVES EIGHT)

Baked Red Snapper Yucatan with Olives and Pimentos

Peruvian Braised Duck

Rice and Green Peas

Tropical Fruit Bowl
in Brazilian Syrup

Coffee with Tequilla

WINE: *Chilean White Wine*
ALTERNATE: *California Pinot Chardonnay*

This is a dinner with a South American flavor. The perfect cocktail for this party would be ice-cold Margueritas.

○

BAKED RED SNAPPER YUCATAN
WITH OLIVES AND PIMENTOS

3 tablespoons butter
1 medium-size mild purple onion
1 clove garlic, peeled
¼ cup coarsely chopped sweet fresh red pepper
2 medium-size tomatoes, peeled and chopped
½ cup dry white wine
½ teaspoon salt
Freshly ground black pepper
1 small jar pimento-stuffed olives (7 ounces), drained and
*   cut in half lengthwise*
½ cup orange juice
1 four and a half- to five-pound red snapper
1 small avocado
2 cups shredded lettuce
4 thinly sliced radishes

Preheat oven to 400° F.

Melt the butter in a saucepan. Add the onions, garlic, and red pepper. Sauté until limp. Add the tomatoes and wine. Season lightly with salt and pepper. Bring to a boil, then reduce heat and let simmer very gently for 15 minutes. Stir frequently.

Remove mixture from heat and add olives and orange juice. Remove and discard garlic.

Arrange the fish in a well-greased, long, shallow baking dish and pour the sauce over and around it. Place fish in a preheated 400° F.) oven and bake 25 minutes, basting frequently with the sauce.

Peel the avocado. Remove pit and cut lengthwise into thin slices. Arrange the avocado slices around the fish and bake for about 5 minutes longer, or until the fish flakes easily when touched with a fork.

With two spatulas, transfer fish to serving platter. Place avocado down the center of the fish and pour sauce over surface. Surround with a ring of shredded lettuce and sliced radishes.

NOTE: Cooked fish may be covered and kept warm on an electric hot tray for up to 30 minutes.

⊙

PERUVIAN BRAISED DUCK

This is an especially good dish for "do it yourself" strategy; it actually should be prepared in advance and reheated. Although the recipe seems long, the "telling" takes more than the "doing"; "stove time" is less than 30 minutes.

> 2 four- to four-and-a-half-pound ducks
> ½ cup fresh lemon juice
> ½ cup fresh lime juice
> ¾ teaspoon cumin seed
> ½ teaspoon salt
> ½ teaspoon freshly ground black pepper
> ¾ cup corn or peanut oil
> 4 bottles (12-ounce size) light beer
> 2 tablespoons chopped parsley

If the ducks are frozen, defrost completely before beginning this dish. Cut each duck into 8 serving pieces, trimming off all excess fat. Combine lemon and lime juice with cumin seed, salt, and pepper in a large nonmetal bowl, add duck pieces, and marinate, covered, in refrigerator for 6 to 8 hours.

Heat oil in a large nonmetal pot (enamelized cast iron is best) until oil is almost sizzling. Dry duck pieces thoroughly with paper towels, then brown them, a few pieces at a time, in the hot oil. Do not try to brown more than 3 or 4 pieces at once, as too many will lower the temperature of the oil and the duck will not brown.

When all the duck pieces are brown, pour off all remaining oil in pot. Return duck pieces and pour in the beer. Turn heat up and bring to a rolling boil, scraping up brown bits that cling to the sides and bottom of the pan. Lower the heat to simmer and allow the duck to cook slowly until tender, about 30 to 40 minutes. Remove duck from liquid to a refrigerator storage dish, cover, and refrigerate. Turn up heat under pot and bring liquid to a boil, boiling rapidly until it is reduced to about 1½ cups. Cool to room temperature, then cover and refrigerate for at least 3 to 4 hours, or until fat has risen to the surface and congealed. Remove fat and discard. About 1 hour before serving, bring stock to a boil, add duck pieces, and heat thoroughly. When ready to serve, pile freshly cooked rice and peas (recipe, page 24) in a serving dish and pour sauce over them. Arrange duck pieces on top of the vegetables and sprinkle with parsley immediately before passing dish to guests.

⊙

RICE AND PEAS

1 10-ounce-package frozen peas
3 cups water
1 teaspoon salt
1 tablespoon corn or safflower oil
1 cup long grain brown rice
2 teaspoons butter at room temperature

Take frozen peas from package and let thaw at room temperature while preparing rice.

Bring the water to a full boil. Add salt, oil and rice. Let boil hard for 2 or 3 minutes then reduce heat and let simmer until rice is tender, about 35 minutes. Pour off any remaining water. Add peas and stir gently with a fork to blend. Add butter, lifting up rice and peas so that it is on the bottom of the pan. Cover pan and place over moderate heat for 10 minutes. Do not uncover but remove pan from heat and let stand in a warm place for 15 to 20 minutes before serving.

NOTE: Rice and peas will remain hot enough to serve for 30 to 45 minutes; or can be transferred to an oven casserole and reheated in a 350° F. oven.

⊙

TROPICAL FRUIT BOWL
IN BRAZILIAN SYRUP

1 coconut
1 pineapple
1 small melon (cantaloupe or honeydew)
2 large seedless oranges
2 bananas
Juice from ½ lime
Brazilian Syrup

To prepare coconut, puncture two of the three soft spots at the top of the coconut and pour off the milk. Place the empty coconut in a preheated 400° F. oven for 15 minutes. When cool enough to handle, tap the entire surface with a hammer until the skin cracks and falls off. Pare off the brown skin and grate the meat.

To prepare the pineapple, cut a thick slice from the top and bottom of the fruit and stand it on a cutting board. With a heavy sharp knife, cut off the peel from the top downward. Turn the pineapple on its side and cut it into slices. Lay the slices flat and cut away all brown "eye" edges. Cut each slice into four wedges and cut away the core part. Cut wedges into bite-size pieces.

Cut melon in half. Scoop out and discard seeds. Cut each half into wedges and cut wedges into bite-size pieces.

Peel oranges. Cut in half and break halves into sections.

Peel and slice bananas.

Combine grated coconut and fruit in a large nonmetal bowl. Add lime juice and toss to blend. Add Brazilian Syrup and blend well. Cover and refrigerate.

For best flavor, remove fruit from refrigerator and let stand at room temperature for about 30 minutes before serving.

BRAZILIAN SYRUP
½ cup sugar
¾ cup water
½ cup light white rum

Combine sugar and water in a saucepan. Cook, stirring, over low heat until sugar dissolves. Let simmer over low heat for 5 minutes. Remove from heat and add rum. Cool to room temperature.

Pour Syrup over any fresh fruit.

Refrigerate sauced fruit for 1 or 2 hours before serving.

○

SEATED DINNER #4
(SERVES EIGHT)

Basque Salad

*London Broil with Wine Merchant Sauce and Fresh
Watercress Garnish*

Very Special Stuffed Baked Potatoes

Baked Stuffed Apple with Cognac Cream

Café Espresso

WINE: *Bordeaux St. Emilion*

○

BASQUE SALAD

3 large green peppers
2 large yellow or red sweet peppers
½ cup olive oil
¼ cup fresh lemon juice
¼ teaspoon fresh or dried tarragon
½ teaspoon chopped parsley
2 tablespoons minced green onions
1 teaspoon sugar
¼ teaspoon salt
¼ teaspoon freshly ground black pepper
4 medium-size ripe tomatoes
16 black Italian or Greek olives
Fresh parsley

Cut peppers into thin strips, removing seeds and white membrane. Heat the oil to medium and sauté the peppers over a low flame for 2 or 3 minutes or until they are slightly soft. Pour oil and peppers into a nonmetal bowl and add lemon juice, tarragon, parsley, green onions, sugar, salt, and pepper. Stir to blend. Refrigerate, covered, for 2 to 3 hours. Peel and seed the tomatoes and slice them into thin rounds. (To peel tomatoes, plunge them briefly into boiling water, then prick with a sharp knife. Skin will slip off easily.) Arrange pepper strips over tomato slices and garnish salad with olives and parsley sprigs.

○

LONDON BROIL
WITH WINE MERCHANT SAUCE

Surprisingly enough, London Broil is not tricky to serve at a party. It actually tastes better if allowed to stand for 20 to 30 minutes after broiling. This is simply because meat that is cut when it is too hot loses all its juices and the result is a dry, tasteless piece of beef. Letting it stand for a bit before carving seals in the juices and the flavor. Just before dinner is announced, when the first course is on the table, the host or hostess can whisk into the kitchen and slice the meat. Now, that problem solved, we can get on with the cooking.

> *3- to 3½-pound London broil or beef flank, preferably*
> *2 to 3 inches thick*
> *1 teaspoon salt*
> *1 teaspoon freshly ground black pepper*

Take the meat from the refrigerator at least 3 hours before cooking, to allow it to come completely to room temperature. Preheat oven to full broil (this means at least 500° F.). Place the meat on a rack about 2 inches from the flame. Broil about 6 to 7 minutes on each side for rare, which is as it should be. London Broil becomes very tough when cooked medium or well done.

Remove from broiler and allow meat to stand in a warm place for 20 to 30 minutes before carving in diagonal slices.

NOTE: The trick here is to have the meat at room temperature and the oven blazing hot.

WINE MERCHANT SAUCE

1 tablespoon butter
2 tablespoons chopped shallots
1 teaspoon flour
½ cup meat stock, fresh or canned
½ cup dry red wine
1 teaspoon tarragon vinegar
Salt
Pepper
½ cup heavy cream
Juices from steak after it has been sliced
2 tablespoons chopped parsley

Melt the butter in the top half of a double boiler. Add the shallots and sauté until limp. Stir in flour, then stock, wine, and vinegar. Let simmer over low heat until mixture is reduced to about ½ cup. Season lightly with salt and pepper.

NOTE: Recipe may be made ahead to this point. Reheat before proceeding.

Add cream, stir to blend, and cook, stirring, until sauce is steamy hot. Stir in steak juices. Blend and pour over steak slices. Garnish with chopped parsley.

May be kept hot over, *not in,* hot water after adding cream. Add steak juices immediately before serving.

⊙

VERY SPECIAL STUFFED BAKED POTATOES

8 medium-size Idaho potatoes
3 tablespoons butter
8 shallots, peeled and minced
½ teaspoon Tabasco sauce
1 teaspoon salt
1 cup cottage cheese, at room temperature
½ cup Parmesan cheese
2 tablespoons chopped parsley

Bake the potatoes until soft and set aside until cool enough to handle. Melt the butter in a small saucepan. Sauté the shallots in the butter over low flame until soft but not brown. Cut the tops off the potatoes and scoop out the insides into a large bowl. Add the sautéed shallots, Tabasco sauce, salt, cottage and Parmesan cheese. Blend well, pile into potato skins, and bake in a moderate oven (350° F.) until very hot and lightly browned. Dust with parsley immediately before serving.

⊙

BAKED STUFFED APPLES
WITH COGNAC CREAM

¼ *cup cognac or other good brandy*
¼ *cup raisins*
8 *large McIntosh apples*
½ *cup brown sugar*
½ *cup chopped walnuts*
2 *tablespoons finely chopped preserved ginger*
1 *cup water mixed with 2 tablespoons white sugar*
Butter

Place raisins in a small bowl and pour cognac over them. Let stand 30 minutes at room temperature.

Preheat oven to 375° F.

Wash apples. Remove core to ½ inch of bottoms and cut a strip of peel from the hollowed ends.

Combine raisins, cognac, brown sugar, walnuts, and ginger. Spoon some of this mixture into the center of each apple.

Place apples in a long, shallow baking pan and pour sugared water around them.

Place a generous pat of butter on top of each apple. Cover pan, place in preheated oven, and bake 30 to 40 minutes or until soft but not mushy. Baste several times after removing from oven. Cover and keep at room temperature until ready to serve. Baste occasionally.

Place apples in small shallow glass bowls and spoon Cognac Cream (recipe below) over each apple just before serving.

COGNAC CREAM

½ pint whipping cream
½ cup confectioners sugar
2 tablespoons cognac or other good brandy

Whip cream until stiff. Fold in sugar, then cognac.

For best and fastest results, use a wire whisk for beating cream and chill both whisk and bowl before you begin. Take cream, cold, from refrigerator and place in freezer for about 15 minutes before beating.

⊙

SEATED DINNER #5
(SERVES EIGHT)

Artichoke Hearts with Red Caviar

Chicken Cecile

Fluffy White Rice

Watermelon Bowl

Coffee with Rum

WINE: *White Burgundy*
ALTERNATE: *Pouilly-Fuissé*

⊙

ARTICHOKE HEARTS WITH RED CAVIAR

This is an appetizer to prepare early in the morning on the day of the party, or even the day before. It tastes far better for the "standing."

2 boxes frozen artichoke hearts
1 jar (4 ounces) red caviar
4 tablespoons homemade mayonnaise (page 71)
2 tablespoons fresh lemon juice
1 tablespoon finely chopped chives
1 teaspoon sugar
¼ teaspoon salt
¼ teaspoon black pepper

Cook artichoke hearts according to package directions. Drain into a nonmetal mixing bowl. Combine remaining ingredients and blend well. Pour over artichoke hearts and stir until mixture is evenly distributed. Cover and refrigerate until ready to serve—at least 4 hours.

⊙

CHICKEN CECILE

It is impossible not to make this heavenly chicken ahead of time. The stock, which is the secret of its exceptional flavor, must be made and then refrigerated until the fat can be removed. And the finished dish tastes even better if refrigerated and then reheated before serving.

> 2 one-and-a-half- to two-pound chickens, ask butcher to
>   cut them Southern style into 8 pieces
> 3 carrots, peeled and cut in half
> 2 small white onions, peeled
> 2 stalks celery
> 2 or 3 sprigs parsley
> 1 cup dry white wine
> 8 cups water
> 1 cup flour
> 1 teaspoon salt
> 1 teaspoon black pepper
> 2 cups salad oil
> 3 tablespoons butter
> 3 tablespoons flour
> 1 small can (4 ounces) whole mushrooms
> 1 cup heavy cream
> ½ cup dry vermouth
> Salt to taste

Place the wings, back pieces, and giblets of the chickens in a large, heavy kettle. Add the carrots, onions, celery, parsley, white wine, and water. Bring to a boil over high heat, skim off foam, lower heat, and cook 3 to 4 hours. Stock should be reduced to about 3 cups of liquid. Strain and discard chicken pieces and vegetables. Refrigerate remaining liquid until fat has risen to the surface and hardens. Remove and discard fat.

Combine the cup of flour, salt, and pepper. Roll chicken pieces in mixture until evenly and lightly coated. Heat the salad oil in a deep, heavy sauté pan until almost smoking. Brown the chicken pieces a few at a time to prevent lowering the temperature of the oil; otherwise the chicken will not brown properly. As the pieces are browned, remove them to paper toweling and drain. When all chicken pieces are brown, pour off and discard any fat remaining in the pan. Heat the butter in the same pan over low heat. Add 3 tablespoons of flour and cook, stirring constantly for 2 or 3 minutes. Add a small amount of the chicken stock, a little at a time, stirring to blend. When it is smooth and lump free, add the remaining chicken stock and stir until well blended. Add the cream and vermouth. Return the chicken pieces to the pan and add mushrooms. Cover and cook over medium heat until chicken is tender, about 30 to 45 minutes. Cover, cool, and refrigerate until about 1 hour before serving. Bring to room temperature and reheat over low heat for 10 to 15 minutes or until thoroughly hot.

⊙

WATERMELON BOWL

This is a refreshing dessert that may be prepared as much as two or three days ahead. It's the perfect answer for any dinner where the entrée is fairly substantial, such as our Chicken Cecile with rice.

1 cup sugar
1 cup water
8 red or purple plums, pitted
6 ripe peaches
1 pint blueberries
¼ cup cognac
1 small watermelon, preferably the round "icebox" type
6 or 8 sprigs mint (optional)

Combine sugar and water in a large nonmetal saucepan and bring to a boil. Wash plums and add to the boiling liquid. Cook briefly for 1 or 2 minutes, then remove pan from heat.

Dip peaches into boiling water for a moment and slip off skins. Cut peach slices directly into the still-hot syrup. Wash blueberries and add to syrup. Stir in cognac. Cover and refrigerate mixture until well chilled.

Cut a thin slice off the bottom of the watermelon so that it will stand firmly. Cut off the top of the melon and scoop out pulp into a large bowl. With a sharp knife cut small "Vs" evenly around the edge of the lower half to give a decorative finish. Slice the pulp into bite-size cubes, discarding seeds. Return the cubed melon to the shell, add chilled fruit mixture to melon, and decorate with mint sprigs. Wrap in foil and refrigerate until ready to serve.

⊙

SEATED DINNER #6
(SERVES EIGHT)

Italian Salad with Garlic Croutons

Beef à la Provençal

Crusty French Bread

Pineapple au Kirsch with Lemon Sherbet

Café Espresso with Lemon Peel

WINE: *Red Burgundy Côte de Nuits*

⊙

ITALIAN SALAD WITH GARLIC CROUTONS

½ *cup olive oil*
¼ *cup wine vinegar*
1 *clove garlic, peeled*
¼ *teaspoon salt*
1 *teaspoon sugar*
1 *teaspoon black pepper*
2 *heads Boston lettuce*
8 *scallions*
8 *small Italian pickled red peppers*
16 *small cherry tomatoes*
8 *slices hard Italian salami, cut in strips*
16 *black olives, preferably the cured-in-olive-oil type*
1 *cup garlic-flavored croutons*
8 *anchovies*

Combine oil, vinegar, garlic, salt, sugar, and pepper in a non-metal bowl. Stir until sugar dissolves. Cover and refrigerate until ready to serve.

Wash lettuce and blot dry on paper toweling. Tear lettuce into bite-size pieces and arrange in individual salad bowls, garnishing each bowl with a whole scallion, two cherry tomatoes, strips of salami, and black olives. Sprinkle with croutons and top with an anchovy. Cover bowls tightly with plastic wrap and refrigerate until ready to serve. Remove garlic clove from dressing and spoon dressing over salads immediately before serving.

○

BEEF À LA PROVENÇAL

This dish makes use of the same basic principle used in the preparation of Chicken Cecile (page 31): the use of a clear, fat-free stock as a cooking liquid that greatly enhances the flavor while lowering the calorie count. Properly done, Beef à la Provençal may be served cold, surrounded by its own beef jelly, but I prefer it hot with plenty of good French bread to mop up the sauce.

3 to 4 pounds beef marrow bones
1 veal knuckle
1 pig's foot
3 white onions, peeled
3 carrots, peeled and cut in half
2 stalks celery
1 small bunch parsley
1 bay leaf
1 teaspoon salt
1 teaspoon black pepper
2 cups dry red wine
½ pound salt pork
1 three- to four-pound pot roast
3 tomatoes, coarsely chopped
6 tablespoons butter
8 to 10 small white onions, peeled
8 to 10 carrots, peeled and cut in half
6 to 8 whole mushrooms
2 tablespoons fresh parsley

Preheat oven to 450° F.

Put the beef bones and the veal knuckle in a large nonmetal pot (enamelized cast iron is best) and place uncovered in preheated oven for 25 to 30 minutes or until bones are brown and crusty. Turn bones once or twice to insure even browning.

Remove pot from oven and place over direct heat on top of the stove. Fill pot with cold water to about 3 inches of the rim. Add pig's foot, the 3 onions, 3 carrots, celery, small bunch of parsley, bay leaf, salt, pepper, and 1 cup of the wine. Bring stock to a boil over high heat, then turn heat to lowest possible setting. Allow stock just barely to simmer for 6 to 8 hours, adding more water if necessary to keep bones covered. When the bone marrow is quite soft and the veal knuckle has separated, the stock is ready.

Strain the stock into a nonmetal bowl, push marrow out of bones with a small knife, and add to stock. Discard bones, pig's foot, and vegetables. Refrigerate mixture for 5 to 6 hours or overnight. Remove congealed fat and refrigerate again.

Wash the salt pork under cold running water to remove surface salt. Pat pork dry with paper toweling and cut into small dice. Place pork pieces in a large, heavy pot—use the same one used for making stock—and fry over very low heat until pork dice are crisp and brown. Remove dice and discard. There should be enough pork fat to cover the bottom of the pot evenly with about ⅛ inch of fat. If not, add a small quantity of salad oil. Have the pot roast at room temperature, heat the fat to almost smoking, and brown the meat on all sides, using two wooden spoons to turn. Do not prick the meat with a fork or the juices will be released and the roast will be dry. When the meat is a dark mahogany color, remove to a platter and reserve. Add the prepared stock, the remaining cup of red wine, and the chopped tomatoes to the pan, bring to a full boil, then lower to simmer. Return the meat to the pot and cook over very low heat for about 25 to 30 minutes to the pound. The liquid should just barely bubble; if it boils, the meat will be tough and tasteless.

While the meat is cooking, melt the butter in a saucepan and lightly brown the rest of the onions and carrots. Remove and set aside. Sauté the mushrooms in the remaining butter for 2 or 3 minutes.

About 30 minutes before the meat is done, add the browned onions, carrots, and sautéed mushrooms. When vegetables are just barely tender, remove meat and vegetables to a covered refrigerator dish, spoon 2 or 3 tablespoons of the stock over them, cover tightly, and refrigerate. Turn up the heat under the stock and boil rapidly until it is reduced to about 4 cups of liquid and has a glazed, "shiny" look. Allow mixture to cool, then pour it into a covered refrigerator dish and chill until fat congeals and rises to the surface. Remove and discard fat.

NOTE: At this point the stock will have jellied and can be served with the cold meat and vegetables. If it is to be served this way, slice the meat and arrange on a platter with the cooked vegetables. Break up the jellied stock with a fork, pile into lettuce cups, and serve on the same platter.

TO SERVE HOT: Heat the stock to boiling, add meat and vegetables, lower heat to simmer, and cook for about 10 minutes to heat thoroughly.

⊙

PINEAPPLE AU KIRSCH
WITH LEMON SHERBET

1 medium- to large-size pineapple
1 tablespoon sugar
½ cup Kirsch
1 quart lemon sherbet

Cut pineapple into thick slices. Cut away peel and dark spots. Slice into bite-size pieces, discarding tough center core. Combine pineapple, sugar, and Kirsch in a nonmetal bowl. Refrigerate for at least 4 to 6 hours. Spoon over lemon sherbet just before serving.

Extra-easy Dinner Parties

⊙

Although it is certainly possible and even easy to serve a five-course dinner on your own, it does take a bit of planning and preparation. There are times when it is pleasant to have a few friends in for a sociable dinner that you would like to keep extra easy.

The following six menus, keyed to the seasons, are just that —the entire meal can be prepared hours in advance and reheated easily. Moreover, you do not have to leave the table at all to serve the meal—and that does make for a relaxed evening for you as well as for your guests.

PARTY STRATEGY

The party strategy is simple. You will need a two-shelf table or serving cart; the top shelf will hold the entrée plates. The entrée itself is placed in front of the host before dinner is served. (Each entrée is planned to stay hot in a covered container while guests are eating their first course.)

An appetizer or soup is on the table when guests are seated, and the dessert is ready and waiting on the lower shelf of the table or serving cart. As before, dessert spoons and forks are laid parallel above the service plates. Wine is either on the table in a wine basket or, if it is to be chilled, in an ice-filled bucket near the host.

⊙

DINNER PARTY FOR FALL
(SERVES EIGHT)

Baked Crab-stuffed Mushrooms

English Steak and Kidney Pie

Watercress and Endive Salad

Caramel Coconut Custard with Rum Ice Cream Sauce

Coffee

WINE: *Red Burgundy Clos St. Denis*

O

BAKED CRAB-STUFFED MUSHROOMS

24 large mushrooms
2 tablespoons olive oil
4 tablespoons butter
½ cup finely minced green onion
4 tablespoons Madeira or a good-quality brandy
2 tablespoons minced parsley
1½ cups flaked crabmeat
¾ cup fine dry bread crumbs
¾ cup heavy cream (more if needed)
1 tablespoon Dijon (or similar) mustard
Salt
White pepper
¼ cup Parmesan cheese
1 tablespoon corn or safflower oil
Paprika
Butter slivers (about 3 tablespoons butter)

Remove stems from mushroom caps by gently bending them back and forth until they snap free. If any part of stems remains, cut it away with the point of a sharp knife.

Rinse stems under cold running water. Drain and pat them dry with paper toweling. Chop as finely as possible.

Wipe mushroom caps clean with a damp cloth and brush them with olive oil.

Melt the 4 tablespoons of butter in a small skillet. Add the green onion and sauté until limp. Add the chopped mushroom stems and cook, stirring, over fairly high heat until they have given off all moisture and turned light brown. Add the cognac and stir until all liquid has cooked away.

Scrape the entire contents of the skillet into a large mixing bowl. Add the parsley, the crabmeat, and ½ cup of the bread crumbs. Stir in the cream and the mustard. Blend well and add more cream if needed but no more than a teaspoonful at a time. (Mixture should be pliable but not too moist.)

Stuff the caps, mounding them high.

Combine the remaining bread crumbs with the Parmesan cheese and sprinkle over mushrooms.

Grease a long, shallow baking pan with the oil and arrange the stuffed mushrooms on it. Sprinkle each with paprika and cover with a sliver of butter.

NOTE: Recipe may be prepared ahead to this point. Leave at room temperature for 1 hour before baking, or refrigerate 4 to 6 hours and then bring to room temperature before baking.

Bake in a preheated 375° F. oven for 15 minutes or until mushrooms are tender. Slide under broiler heat briefly to brown the tops.

NOTE: This dish may be served as a before-dinner appetizer with cocktails.

⊙

ENGLISH STEAK AND KIDNEY PIE

¼ pound salt pork
1½ pounds top round of beef, cut into 1-inch cubes
Flour
Salt
Pepper
3 tablespoons butter
1 large onion, chopped
2 cups beef stock, fresh or canned
1 cup dry red wine
16 tiny white onions, peeled
4 veal kidneys
¼ cup cognac or other good-quality brandy
2 teaspoons Worcestershire sauce
Salt, if needed
Pepper, if needed
dough for top pie crust

Cut salt pork into small dice. Cover with water and bring to a boil. Lower heat and let pieces simmer for 5 minutes, then drain and pat dry. Place pork dice in a large, heavy skillet and fry over low heat until all fat has been rendered and pork dice are crisp.

Remove them with a slotted spoon and drain on paper toweling. Set aside.

Roll the beef cubes in flour heavily seasoned with salt and pepper. Shake off excess flour.

Pour all but about 2 tablespoons of the rendered fat from the skillet into a small bowl.

Heat remaining fat to almost smoking. Add a few beef cubes and cook, turning until meat is browned on all sides. Using a slotted spoon, remove beef cubes as soon as browned. Add additional fat as needed and continue to cook meat a few cubes at a time until all are browned.

Pour off all fat from the skillet and add 1 tablespoon of the butter. When melted, add the chopped onion and sauté until limp. Return the meat to the skillet and add the stock and wine. Cover skillet and cook over very low heat until meat is tender—about 1½ hours. Remove from heat.

While meat cooks, parboil onions for 10 minutes or until almost tender. Drain.

Wash the kidneys, cut in half, and remove the cores. Cut into cubes.

Melt the remaining butter in a second skillet over medium heat. Add the kidney cubes and cook, stirring gently, for about 3 minutes. Increase the heat to high, pour in the cognac, and ignite. Let flame briefly. Remove from heat and let flame subside.

Reheat meat, sauce, and onions. Add Worcestershire sauce and correct seasoning, if needed, with salt and pepper. Arrange meat, veal kidneys, onions, and sauce in a lightly buttered 2-quart casserole.

Preheat oven to 400° F.

Cover the casserole with rolled-out pastry dough. Press edges of dough down with a fork and make a few gashes in the top.

Place in the preheated oven and bake for about 25 minutes or until crust is lightly browned.

NOTE: Recipe may be made ahead to this point.

Refrigerate, covered. About 1 hour before baking, remove from refrigerator and let stand at room temperature, then place in a 350° F. oven until heated. Proceed with recipe.

○

CARAMEL COCONUT CUSTARD
WITH RUM ICE CREAM SAUCE

6 egg yolks
½ pint heavy cream
1 pint milk
1 cup sugar
2 tablespoons dark rum
2 tablespoons finely grated coconut

Preheat oven to 350° F.

Place egg yolks in a large mixing bowl and beat until well blended.

Combine cream and milk in a saucepan over moderate heat until steamy. Remove from heat and set aside.

Caramelize the sugar in a second heavy saucepan—preferably one of enamelized cast iron—by stirring over medium heat until it turns to a light golden syrup. Slowly add the still-warm cream and milk, stirring as it is added. Cook, stirring, until caramelized sugar has dissolved completely.

Remove from heat and add the mixture to the beaten egg yolks, beating with a wire whisk as it is added. Stir in the rum and coconut. Blend well. Pour into a 2-quart soufflé mold. Place mold in a larger pan and pour enough hot water around it to come about halfway up the sides of the mold. Place in the preheated oven and bake for 1 hour or until firm. (A good test of firmness is when a knife inserted in the center comes out clean.)

Refrigerate until thoroughly chilled, 3 hours or longer.

Spoon chilled custard into dessert bowls and top with **Rum Ice Cream Sauce** (recipe below).

NOTE: The coconut rises to the surface of the custard to form a light and delicious crust.

RUM ICE CREAM SAUCE
1 pint French vanilla ice cream
¼ cup dark rum

Place frozen ice cream in a mixing bowl and let stand at room temperature until soft but not melted. Add rum and blend well. Refreeze until one hour before serving, let stand at room temperature until soft enough to spoon over custard.

Serve over any mild sweet custard or cake.

☉

LATE-SUMMER DINNER PARTY
(SERVES EIGHT)

Country Vegetable Soup

Cold Lemon Roast Chicken with Cumberland Sauce

Corn Pudding

Blueberries with Sour Cream

Iced Tea

☉

COUNTRY VEGETABLE SOUP

¼ pound salt pork, diced
2½ quarts beef stock, fresh or canned
3 medium potatoes, peeled and quartered
2 carrots, scraped and cut in half
2 medium onions, peeled and quartered
1 white turnip, peeled and quartered
3 tablespoons minced parsley
3 sprigs fresh thyme
1 teaspoon salt
½ teaspoon pepper
1 cup corn kernels, fresh or frozen
½ small green cabbage, finely shredded

Blanch the pork by boiling it in a small amount of water for 3 or 4 minutes; drain and pat dry. Fry the pork in a 4- to 5-quart soup pot over low heat until the meat is crisp and lightly browned. Remove pork with slotted spoon and drain on paper towels. Set aside and reserve.

Pour off and discard all but about 1 tablespoon of the rendered fat. Add all remaining ingredients except the corn and cabbage. Bring soup to boiling, then lower heat so that soup barely simmers. Skim liquid once or twice and continue to cook over lowest possible heat for 2 to 3 hours or until vegetables are very soft. Remove vegetables with a slotted spoon and puree in an electric blender or press through a food mill. Return the pureed vegetables to the soup and blend well; it should be quite thick.

NOTE: At this point the soup can be refrigerated, well covered, until about 1 hour before serving. Let stand at room temperature for 30 minutes before reheating.

Bring the soup to boiling, add the cabbage and corn, and cook over medium heat for 10 to 15 minutes. Garnish with the pork bits and serve with crusty French bread.

NOTE: If the soup becomes too thick at any point, add a small amount of boiling water—just enough to make it "pourable." It is traditionally a very thick soup.

⊙

COLD LEMON ROAST CHICKEN
WITH CUMBERLAND SAUCE

1 four- to five-pound roasting chicken
Salt
Pepper
½ cup melted butter
3 tablespoons fresh lemon juice
Parsley sprigs or watercress for garnish

Preheat oven to 350° F.

Have chicken at room temperature. Rub well inside and out with salt and pepper. Combine melted butter and lemon juice and brush chicken with the mixture, using a pastry brush. Place chicken on rack in preheated oven and roast for approximately 1 hour, basting frequently with lemon-and-butter mixture. Turn the chicken from time to time to ensure even browning. To test the chicken for doneness, prick the thigh with a sharp pointed knife; if the liquid that runs out is clear and the thigh bone moves easily, the bird is done.

Let the chicken stand for at least 10 to 15 minutes at room

temperature, then carve into serving-size portions and arrange on serving platter. Refrigerate, tightly covered, until about 1 hour before serving. Bring to room temperature and garnish with parsley or watercress. Serve with Cumberland Sauce (recipe below).

CUMBERLAND SAUCE
1 cup currant jelly
2 teaspoons Dijon mustard
1 tablespoon grated lemon peel
1 tablespoon grated orange peel
Juice of medium-size lemon
Juice of small orange
1 tablespoon cognac (optional)

Melt the jelly over very low heat and combine it with remaining ingredients. Chill mixture until ready to serve, then break it up with a fork before pouring it into a serving dish.

Makes about 1¼ cups sauce.

⊙

CORN PUDDING

3 eggs
2 cups heavy cream
3 cups fresh corn, cut from the cob
½ teaspoon sugar
½ teaspoon salt
½ teaspoon pepper
Paprika

Beat the eggs lightly and combine them with all remaining ingredients except paprika. Pour mixture into a buttered soufflé mold.

NOTE: At this point the pudding may be refrigerated, well covered, until about 2 hours before serving. It should be brought to room temperature before baking.

Bake the pudding for about 1 hour or until a knife inserted in the center comes out clean. Dust with paprika and serve from the baking dish.

⊙

WINTER DINNER PARTY

Clear Beef Broth with Marrow, French Bread, and Grated Cheese

Boiled Beef with Vegetables

Horseradish Sauce

Gherkins

Munster Cheese and Crisp Apple Slices

Applesauce Cake Squares

Coffee

Imported German Beer

⊙

CLEAR BEEF BROTH WITH MARROW, FRENCH BREAD, AND GRATED CHEESE

8 cups beef stock (Boiled Beef recipe, page 47)
Salt
Marrow from beef bones (Boiled Beef recipe, page 47)
8 thick slices French bread
1 cup grated Gruyère cheese

Heat stock to boiling. Dice marrow and add it to hot stock. Correct seasoning with salt. Place one slice of bread in each soup bowl. Pour stock over bread.

Place cheese in a small bowl and pass it around the table.

⊙

BOILED BEEF
WITH VEGETABLES

1 five-pound piece of beef, rump or bottom round
3 pounds beef marrow bones
2 cloves garlic, peeled and cut in slivers (optional)
1 veal knuckle bone
4 quarts boiling water
2 teaspoons salt
1 carrot, scraped
1 large onion stuck with 2 cloves
6 parsley sprigs
6 celery tops with leaves
1 bay leaf
6 pepper corns
1 teaspoon thyme
16 baby carrots, scraped, or 8 carrots cut into 2-inch pieces
16 tiny white onions
Salt to taste
Freshly ground black pepper to taste

Ask your butcher to tie the meat securely so that it will not fall apart while cooking. Have the beef marrow bones sawed into 3-inch pieces.

With a small, sharp knife, make 6 or 8 incisions in the meat; into each cut, insert a sliver of garlic. This step is optional but the flavor of the garlic will not be strong when the meat is cooked and it does add character.

Place meat, beef marrow bones, and veal knuckle in a large, heavy 8- to 10-quart stockpot and add the boiling water. (Hot water seals the juices in as effectively as searing the meat in hot fat.)

Bring meat and bones to a boil and skim surface until clear. Add remaining ingredients, lower heat, and let simmer for about 2½ hours or until the meat is almost, but not quite, done. A fork will pierce the meat easily but meets a slight resistance.

Remove the meat to a nonmetal storage dish. Remove marrow bones and set aside.

Strain stock through a fine sieve.

Wash out the stockpot thoroughly, then return the meat to it and pour in the strained stock. Refrigerate 6 hours or longer.

With a small, sharp knife, scoop out the marrow from the bones and place marrow in a glass storage dish. Add a little stock, cover, and refrigerate until ready to use. Discard the bones.

NOTE: Recipe may be made ahead to this point.

Remove stockpot from refrigerator. Remove and discard all congealed fat from the surface of the meat and stock. Bring to a boil, then lower heat and add carrots and onions. Let simmer until vegetables and meat are tender—about 20 minutes. Don't overcook the vegetables. If they are done before the meat, remove them from the stock. Continue to cook the meat as long as necessary, then return vegetables to the pot until reheated.

Slice and arrange the meat on a serving platter. Surround with carrots and onions. Spoon a little of the hot stock over both meat and vegetables.

Place platter on an electric hot tray or in a warming oven.

Heat stock to boiling. Dice and add reserved marrow.

Serve stock as a first course, then serve meat and vegetables.

NOTE: Boiled beef reheats perfectly and actually improves in flavor if made one or two days in advance, but the accompanying carrots and onions are at their best if they are cooked just before serving.

Leftover stock may be stored, covered, in the refrigerator to be used as the base for soups, stews, or casseroles. Reheated to boiling every 4 or 5 days, it can be kept for about 4 weeks in the refrigerator, or it may be frozen and stored, securely wrapped, in the freezer for 6 weeks to 2 months.

Cover any leftover meat with stock and store, covered, in refrigerator. It is delicious served cold.

⊙

APPLESAUCE CAKE SQUARES

3¼ cups all-purpose flour
2 teaspoons baking soda
¼ teaspoon salt
2 cups chopped pecans
3 cups raisins
½ cup (1 stick) butter, at room temperature
¾ cup dark brown sugar, firmly packed
2 eggs, well beaten
2 cups canned applesauce
2 tablespoons dark rum

Preheat oven to 325° F.

Grease a baking pan, 12 inches by 8 inches by 2 inches, with oil. Sprinkle with flour and shake pan to distribute flour evenly.

Sift together 2½ cups of the flour, the baking soda, and salt. Combine remaining flour with the pecans and raisins.

In a large bowl, cream the butter until fluffy. Add the brown sugar and beat until mixture is well blended and light. Beat in the eggs. Add the flour mixture alternating with the applesauce, beating well after each addition. Fold in the pecans and raisins. Pour the batter into the prepared pan and bake in the preheated oven for 45 minutes or until cake is firm. (If cake is firm, a knife plunged into the center will come out clean.)

Cool slightly, then turn out onto a cake rack. Let cake cool completely before cutting it into small squares.

Store extra squares in plastic food bags in the refrigerator.

They will keep in the refrigerator 6 to 7 days, and in the freezer for 2 to 3 months. Bring squares to room temperature again before serving.

Card-table Dinner Parties

⊙

Card-table parties are one of the pleasantest ways to entertain four guests—or forty. Any number can play; only space dictates your limitations. A card-table party is particularly good strategy if your castle is a city apartment with its usual lack of a real dining room, or if your dining table can't comfortably accommodate the number of guests. After dinner, the evening can continue with card playing, or the table(s) can be whisked out of sight for quick transformation back to a living room. If your room is high, wide, and handsome, the cleared space can be used for dancing to anything from a good phonograph to a trio of musicians. Your taste and your pocketbook are the determining factors.

If your party is small—one or two foursomes—you can easily cope with the triple roles of cook, butler, and hostess or host. More than two groups of four need an extra server. With still larger groups, it's best to have one helper for each additional three tables. But regardless of the number of guests, if you use the same basic plan the evening will flow as smoothly as the River Shannon. Here's how:

PARTY PLANNING

After you have invited your guests and selected your menu, your first consideration should be about your tables. If necessary, standard-size card tables can be rented from a party-rental service or a caterer. You can also rent latch-on round tops to fit over them so that each table will seat six if you prefer. Cloths to fit over the tables can often be rented from the same supplier. These, however, more often than not, are plain white and not too fresh-looking, so you may want to have pretty new ones made or make them yourself. In either case, do give yourself ample time. It's a bit hard on the nerves to be frantically sewing—or waiting for someone else to—on the day of your party.

It is also a good idea to set up your tables two or three days before the event to see how they fit into the decor of your rooms. You may have to rearrange your furniture a bit or transfer a few pieces to another part of the house so as not to crowd your tables too closely together. There is no reason to make major changes, however. Your tables can be set up almost anywhere and need not be confined to one room. The idea of dining all over the house has taken over and space stretching is the "in" thing. In fact, it is often those without a dining room at all who give the best parties.

I place my tables wherever it's most pleasant—on the terrace, by a blazing fire in the living room, in the garden, or even in the kitchen. My arrangement depends on the season, the type of party, and the number of tables, but it is always where everyone will be uncrowded, comfortable, and relaxed. The result is that a good time just naturally happens.

Choose two equally pleasant but adjoining sites if you like, indoors and out. Settings for each table need not be identical, just keep them color related.

TABLE DECOR

Table decor is best kept simple. There just isn't any room on a small table for impressive flower arrangements. A single candlestick is nice if it's either tall enough or low enough not to blind the diners. Each cloth and its napkins should complement the setting. Charming, informal flower or patchwork prints are fine in a "countrylike" atmosphere; more formal surroundings call for a less rustic effect. There's no reason why each table should not be covered with a different colored cloth as long as the colors are compatible with the room. They should, however, be of one fabric —three shades of linen or Indian Head cloth can be very effective, for instance.

If your room can take it, from a color standpoint it's a nice idea to use seasonal colors and flowers to match—pale green, yellow and white, or pink for spring with pots of white narcissus, daffodils, and white or pink tulips used around the room. For summer, deep blue cloths with blue-edged white napkins look wonderful with masses of zinnias or pink and white snapdragons arranged in tin-lined wicker baskets. Obviously chrysanthemums can set the tone for fall with gold, bronze, and yellow cloths. Christmas calls for real red or Christmas pink. The first should be used with traditional arrangements of greens and holly; the second, with bare silvered branches hung with small silvery balls. Regardless of your color scheme, however, candles should always be white or pale ivory. A pox on colored candles!

If this sounds expensive, remember that almost anyone can

run up a simple cloth and a few big napkins. The main idea is to create a festive atmosphere. It doesn't take a great deal of money; it needs only creativity and a small amount of planning.

MENU PLANNING

Having solved the problem of your tables, you can return to concentrating on your menu. As with any party, the more you do ahead of time, the easier it becomes. Good parties don't just happen; they are carefully organized. A good way to start is to put all the essentials down on paper. Write out your menu on one side of a large sheet of lined legal paper. Then list all the equipment required to cook and serve each dish. On a second sheet, write the necessary ingredients you will need, right down to such mundane supplies as salt and pepper. Now check your supplies, both equipment and food, and prepare a third list for shopping. Don't forget such extras as cigarettes, matches, ice, cocktail picks, liqueurs, cocktail napkins, etc., in addition to the usual pots, plates, silver, and food. Map out the evening in your mind from the time you open the door for the first guest to the last "good night." It's sure-fire insurance for a good party.

PARTY STRATEGY

Now exactly how are you going to handle your party? Here's how I usually do it:

Cocktail ingredients should be set up on a tray on a side table. Few people like complicated drinks these days. Scotch, gin, vodka, and vermouth should fill most requirements; Southerners add bourbon. A large, well-stocked ice bucket is a necessity, and plan to have ample ice reserves in the kitchen. Add tonic water, sparkling water, and a pitcher of plain water plus one of lemon-spiked tomato juice for nondrinkers. Ice tongs, stirring spoons, a small knife, and a supply of lemons, limes, and oranges are final necessities.

Tables are completely set before guests arrive and the first course is placed on each table over the dinner plate, Palm Beach style, before people are seated. This means the tables are cleared only once during the meal.

After the appetizer is removed, the entrée is brought from the kitchen on a single platter and offered to each guest. The main course concluded, the table is then cleared for dessert and dessert service (service plate and fingerbowl) is brought in. The diner lifts the fingerbowl and places it just above the service plate, then dessert is passed. Individual ash trays with a pretty folder of matches are just above the forks. Wine glasses are above and a little to the right of the entrée knife. Red wine is placed on the table in a wine basket, and white wine should be chilling in an ice bucket near each table.

TABLE SERVICE

All silver is placed on the table before guests are seated, knives and spoons to the right, forks to the left. The dessert spoon and fork are placed horizontally across the table just above the service plates. The diner removes these to the sides of the plate before dessert is served.

Service is laid according to use, with first implements at farthest outside position. Appetizer fork is at far left and appetizer knife is at far right; if soup is being served the soup spoon is to the left of the appetizer knife. Next come entrée fork and knife in inner left and right positions. If you prefer, dessert silver may be placed on the dessert and fingerbowl plate, fork to the right, spoon to the left. The diner then removes them to the sides of the plate and dessert is passed. This is a more formal type of service but it's a little bit more trouble, so unless I have skilled help for the evening, I use the more informal style.

COFFEE AND LIQUEURS

Coffee is served from a tray in the living room while the tables are cleared. I also like to offer guests a liqueur or cognac with their coffee. If you are uncertain about which liqueurs to serve, usually a good French cognac is all you need. Just about everyone who drinks liqueurs likes it.

AFTER DINNER

As for after dinner, I find most people just like to sit and talk, but if your guests are card players, you already have tables set up and the evening can continue with a good game. I always try to have music. Budget permitting, I engage a pianist who brings his own portable electric piano; people often like to gather around and sing after a good meal. As to where to find a pianist, consult your local music store or school, both of which usually have lists as to who is available. If having live music isn't possible, I buy some good new records (no vocals—usually piano music) and just keep it low and soft.

A final note—one of the things that makes a party is fragrance. In addition to having the fresh scent of flowers, just before guests arrive I spray a drop of my favorite perfume on the light bulbs. This gives a wonderfully festive touch to the setting.

⊙

CARD-TABLE DINNER #1
(SERVES EIGHT)

Shrimp-stuffed Artichokes à la Louisiane

Shallot Chicken with Applejack

Rice Pilaf

Glazed Crab Apples and Watercress

Hot Parkerhouse Rolls

Cornelia Drexel's Apricot Meringue Cake

Coffee and Cognac

WINE: *California Pinot Chardonnay*

⊙

SHRIMP-STUFFED ARTICHOKES
À LA LOUISIANE

8 artichokes
Lemon juice
1 tablespoon salt
½ cup melted butter
1 tablespoon finely minced onions
3 tablespoons finely minced celery
1 cup soft fresh fine bread crumbs
½ teaspoon salt
½ pound shrimp, cooked, peeled, and deveined
½ teaspoon pepper
½ teaspoon paprika
1 lightly beaten egg

Trim the stems of the artichokes flat so they will stand up-right, then rub the bottoms with lemon juice. Fill a large bowl or pot with cold water and add salt. Plunge the artichokes up and down in the salted water to remove sand or any debris. Drain. Trim leaves evenly with scissors. Rub all cut portions with lemon juice. Place the artichokes upright in a large kettle. Add water to cover them completely. Cover tightly and bring quickly to a boil over high heat. Cook for 20 minutes or until the leaves can be pulled off and bottoms are just tender. Drain and rinse in cold water to stop cooking process.

Heat 2 tablespoons of the butter in a small frying pan and sauté the onion and celery over low heat until soft but not brown. Combine with bread crumbs in a mixing bowl. Chop the shrimp very fine and add to mixture along with remaining butter, beaten egg, and seasoning.

Mix well to blend. Stuff the artichokes by pushing mixture well down between leaves with a small coffee spoon.

Place stuffed artichokes in a deep ovenproof casserole or Dutch oven so that they fit snugly together or tie with soft string so they retain their shape. Pour in enough boiling water to cover the bottom of the casserole to a depth of about ½ inch. Cover tightly and bake for 15 to 20 minutes. Remove artichokes from casserole, remove string, and place on serving plates. Serve at room temperature.

NOTE: Recipe may be made ahead and refrigerated but artichokes should be at room temperature when served.

⊙

SHALLOT CHICKEN WITH APPLEJACK

2 two-pound broiler chickens
½ cup flour
Salt
White pepper
3 tablespoons oil
3 tablespoons butter
3 tablespoons applejack, warmed
8 shallots, peeled
1 cup chicken stock, fresh or canned
2 tablespoons butter
16 mushrooms
Minced parsley

This dish can be made with larger chickens but the small-size broilers are infinitely preferable. They are more tender, they cook faster, and they have better flavor.

Have your butcher cut each chicken into eight pieces, Southern style, discarding backbone and wing tips. Wash the chicken pieces and dry carefully with paper towels. Combine the flour, salt, and pepper in a large mixing bowl and dip each chicken piece lightly in the mixture. Shake free of excess flour. Heat the oil and the 3 tablespoons of butter in a large, heavy sauté pan, one with a close-fitting lid (enamelized cast iron is best). The oil and butter should be sizzling hot. Brown the chicken, 2 or 3 pieces at a time. More than this will lower the temperature of the oil and the chicken will not brown. Remove the browned pieces to a platter and keep warm.

In the remaining oil in the pan, sauté the shallots over medium heat until golden. Remove with slotted spoon and set aside.

Pour off any remaining oil, return the chicken pieces to the pan, and heat briefly over medium flame. Pour the warmed apple-jack over the chicken pieces and ignite. When the flame subsides, add the sautéed shallots and chicken stock. Cover and cook over very low heat 20 to 25 minutes or until chicken is tender, basting occasionally. While the chicken is cooking, melt the 2 tablespoons of butter in a saucepan and sauté the mushrooms until soft but not limp. About 5 or 10 minutes before chicken is done, add the mushrooms and stir to blend. Remove chicken pieces and mushrooms to a serving platter. Spoon a small amount of sauce over each piece and sprinkle with parsley.

NOTE: This dish may be successfully prepared ahead and re-frigerated until ready to reheat. Reheat, covered, over low heat.

⊙

RICE PILAF

1½ cups fat-free chicken stock, fresh or canned
2 cups water
½ teaspoon salt
1 tablespoon butter
1 tablespoon oil
2 tablespoons minced green onion
1½ cups uncooked rice
¼ teaspoon ground saffron

Combine stock and water in saucepan. Add salt and bring to a boil.

Meanwhile, melt the butter with oil in a second saucepan. Add onions and sauté for one minute. Stir in rice and saffron. Add boiling stock mixture and stir once. Cover and cook without re-moving the lid for 20 minutes. Pour off any remaining water. Cover and place over very low heat for 5 minutes or until rice is fluffy and dry.

○

GLAZED CRAB APPLES

1 cup sugar
¼ cup water
Juice of ½ lemon
Few drops of red food coloring
1 jar (16 ounces) spiced crab apples, drained

Combine sugar, water, and lemon juice in a saucepan. Boil over high heat until syrup begins to thicken. Remove from heat. Stir in food coloring.

Arrange crab apples in a shallow refrigerator dish. Pour syrup over apples. Chill before serving.

○

CORNELIA DREXEL'S
APRICOT MERINGUE CAKE

4 egg whites
½ teaspoon cream of tartar
1 cup powdered sugar, sifted
2 cups stewed sweetened dried apricots
1 tablespoon grated lemon rind
2 cups heavy cream.

Preheat oven to 250° F.

Separate the eggs while they are cold, reserving the yolks for another use. Let the egg whites stand in a large mixing bowl until they reach room temperature. Add the cream of tartar to the egg whites and beat with a wire whisk until mixture is very stiff and almost dry. Gradually beat in ½ cup of the sugar, not more than 1 tablespoon at a time. Continue beating until the meringue is very stiff and glossy. Beat in the vanilla, then sprinkle with the remaining ½ cup of sugar and fold in gently.

Lightly oil two cookie sheets and dust with flour. Draw two

8-inch circles on each of them, using a cake tin as a guide. Spread the circles evenly with meringue. Bake in the preheated oven for about 1 hour or until the meringues have set. Do not allow to brown. Remove from oven and cool away from drafts; then, using a spatula, remove the layers to a clean, flat surface.

Puree the apricots in a blender or put them through a food mill. Combine with lemon rind and blend. One hour before serving, whip the cream until very stiff. Fold half of the stiff cream into the apricots. Assemble the meringue cakes, spreading apricot mixture between the layers. Cover with remaining whipped cream and refrigerate until ready to serve.

○

CARD-TABLE DINNER #2
(SERVES EIGHT)

Leeks Vinaigrette

Veal Marengo with Flat Noodles

Lemon Sherbet Sprinkled with Kirsch and Chopped Fresh Strawberries

Almond Wafers

Espresso

WINE: *Bordeaux St. Emilion*

⊙

LEEKS VINAIGRETTE

24 leeks
2 cloves garlic, peeled and minced
½ cup salad oil
2 cups water (more if needed)
1 teaspoon salt
1 cup white wine vinegar
1 teaspoon freshly ground black pepper
3 tablespoon finely minced parsley
Crisp lettuce leaves
Lemon wedges

Cut off the roots of the leeks but not so deeply as to separate the white leaves. Trim the tops so that each leek is approximately 6 inches long.

Wash leeks carefully to ensure their being free of sand. Spread the green leaves apart and run cold water through them. Soak them, leaves side down, in cold water for 10 minutes, then wash a second time.

Preheat oven to 500° F.

Place leeks in a shallow baking dish just large enough to hold them side by side in a single layer.

Mix together the oil, garlic, water, and salt and pour this over the leeks. Add additional water if needed to almost but not quite cover them.

Cover the baking dish loosely with foil and place it in the preheated oven. Immediately reduce the oven temperature to 350° F. Bake for 30 minutes or until leeks are tender. Turn each leek several times as they bake, using tongs or two spoons.

Remove the dish from the heat and pour the vinegar over the leeks. Sprinkle with pepper and parsley. Cool to room temperature.

Drain the leeks thoroughly. Serve on crisp lettuce leaves and garnish each serving with a thin wedge of lemon.

NOTE: Recipe may be made ahead. Cover and refrigerate in the marinade until about 1 hour before serving. The leeks are best served at room temperature.

⊙

VEAL MARENGO WITH FLAT NOODLES

Named for the northern Italian town of Marengo, this hearty stew of veal, stock, wine, and tomatoes is a classic meal in itself. It has the added advantage of tasting even better when made a day ahead and reheated at serving time.

3 pounds veal rump, cut into 2-inch cubes
¼ pound salt pork
3 tablespoons flour
3 tablespoons butter
¾ cup finely chopped shallots
1½ teaspoons minced garlic
½ teaspoon salt
½ teaspoon freshly ground black pepper
1 tablespoon grated lemon peel
1 tablespoon tomato paste
3 medium-size tomatoes, peeled, seeded, and chopped
3 tablespoons chopped parsley
1 bay leaf, crumbled
1 cup dry white wine
1 cup brown stock, fresh or canned
1 cup fresh mushrooms, chopped
1 pound flat noodles, cooked according to package directions

Preheat oven to 350° F.

Select your veal with care; it should be firm with clear white fat and rosy light pink in color. You will probably get better veal by buying it in one piece and cutting it into cubes yourself. Have the meat at room temperature before beginning.

Cut the salt pork into small dice and blanch in a small amount of boiling water for 2 or 3 minutes. Drain and pat dry.

In a deep, heavy sauté pan, fry the pork dice over low heat until crisp and lightly browned. Remove them with slotted spoon and set aside.

Roll the chunks of veal in the flour until lightly but evenly coated. Heat the pork fat remaining in the pan to almost smoking and brown the meat a few pieces at a time, turning them until they are evenly browned and slightly crusty. Do not attempt to cook more than 3 or 4 pieces at once or you will lower the temperature of the fat and the meat will not brown. If more fat is needed, add a little cooking oil, but be sure to let the mixture heat before adding more meat.

When all the meat pieces are browned, remove them to a platter and keep warm. Discard any remaining oil in the pan and add the butter. When butter is melted, add the shallots and garlic and cook over low heat until soft but not brown. Add the browned meat and all remaining ingredients except the mushrooms. Bring the mixture to a boil over medium heat. Cover and place in the preheated oven. Bake for 1 hour. Add the chopped mushrooms for the last 20 minutes of cooking. Serve at once or refrigerate and reheat when ready to serve. Immediately before serving, sprinkle with crisp pork bits.

The sauce should be quite thick; if it is not, boil it down on top of the stove until reduced to about 2½ cups of sauce. If it is too thick, add a small amount of stock.

Serve over hot flat noodles. If necessary, noodles may be prepared up to 30 minutes before serving. Drain and return to cooking pan. Add 2 tablespoons of butter at room temperature and toss noodles with a fork. Cover and set aside. Reheat briefly over very low heat immediately before serving.

⊙

ALMOND WAFERS

1 cup butter, at room temperature
1½ cups sugar
6 egg yolks
2 teaspoons cognac
2 cups flour
1 cup almonds, blanched and ground

Cream butter until very soft. Add sugar and cream until very fluffy and light. Add egg yolks one at a time, beating after each addition. Beat in cognac. Add flour, a small amount at a time, and beat well. Add almonds and blend. Turn out on a lightly floured

wooden cutting board and shape into a long, narrow roll. (If dough seems too soft to handle, chill it in the refrigerator until slightly firm before turning it out on the board.) Refrigerate or freeze cookie roll. When needed, slice off as many cookies as desired and bake them in a 300° F. oven for 8 to 10 minutes. Cookie roll will keep frozen 2 to 3 three weeks.

Makes about 50 cookies.

○

CARD-TABLE DINNER #3
(SERVES EIGHT)

Tomatoes Stuffed with Rice Salad

Roast Stuffed Leg of Lamb

Puree of Carrots à la Crème

Puree of Peas with Lettuce

Minted Pear Halves

Fresh Strawberry Tarts

Café Filtre

WINE: *California Cabernet Sauvignon*

⊙

TOMATOES STUFFED WITH
RICE SALAD

8 medium-size firm ripe tomatoes
Salt
2 cups cooked rice, well chilled
2 tablespoons minced green onions
1 cup finely chopped celery
1 cup minced lean baked ham
1 teaspoon Dijon mustard
¼ teaspoon curry powder
1 tablespoon mayonnaise (page 71)
¼ cup vinegar
¾ cup mild salad oil
Crisp lettuce leaves

Cut a thin slice off the stem end of each tomato, then hollow out the centers with a small spoon. Reserve the center pulp and juice for another use. Sprinkle the insides of the tomato shells with salt and invert them on paper toweling to drain for about 15 minutes.

Combine the rice, green onions, celery, and ham in a large bowl.

Stir the mustard and curry powder into the mayonnaise. Add the vinegar and salad oil. Beat with a wire whisk until it is well blended and frothy, then pour over rice mixture.

Toss salad gently with two forks to distribute dressing.

NOTE: Recipe may be made ahead to this point. Refrigerate both tomato shells and salad until just before serving.

Fill tomato shells with rice, piling it high.

Serve each tomato on a crisp lettuce leaf.

○

ROAST STUFFED LEG OF LAMB

1 six- to seven-pound leg of lamb, boned
Salt
Pepper
2 tablespoons currant jelly
½ cup butter
2 tablespoons finely chopped onions
2 cups cracker crumbs
1 clove garlic, peeled and minced
½ cup finely chopped parsley
1 lightly beaten egg

Preheat oven to 450° F.

Bring meat to room temperature and place on a flat surface, boned side up. Sprinkle lightly with salt and pepper. Melt the currant jelly in a small saucepan over low heat. Brush bone cavity with melted jelly. Melt the butter in a skillet and sauté the onion and garlic over low heat until soft but not brown.

Remove mixture from heat and add cracker crumbs, parsley, and egg. Mix well to blend. Spread the stuffing into the bone cavity. Roll up the meat and tie with butcher's string. Place the meat on rack in preheated oven and roast for 10 minutes. Turn oven down to 350° F. and continue to roast for approximately 2½ hours or 20 minutes to the pound. Baste frequently with pan juices. Allow the roast to cool for at least 20 minutes before carving into slices.

TO PREPARE AHEAD: Carve the meat, place slices on an oven-proof platter, and baste lightly with pan juices. Cover platter tightly with aluminum foil and place it in a warming oven.

○

PUREE OF CARROTS À LA CRÈME

2 pounds carrots
¼ teaspoon salt
2 tablespoons heavy cream
2 tablespoons butter
¼ cup fine bread crumbs (more if needed)

Wash and scrape the carrots. Slice them into thin rounds and place in a saucepan, one with a tight-fitting lid. Add salt and just enough boiling water to cover. Cover carrots and cook over high heat 10 to 12 minutes or until tender. There should be almost no water left in the pan. Press the carrots through a food mill or puree in a blender. If there is any pan liquid left, add it to the pureed carrots. In the top half of a double boiler, heat the cream very gently until steamy, but *do not boil*. Stir in butter until it melts. Add cream and butter to carrots in a mixing bowl and whip until fluffy. Beat in bread crumbs. If carrots seem too liquid, more bread crumbs may be added. Keep vegetables hot in the top half of a double boiler over hot, but not boiling, water.

○

PUREE OF PEAS WITH LETTUCE

2 packages (10-ounce sizes) frozen peas
2 tablespoon butter, at room temperature
2 tablespoons water
½ teaspoon salt (more if desired)
½ teaspoon sugar
2 tablespoons cream
½ cup Boston lettuce, chopped

Remove frozen peas from package and let them thaw at room temperature for 1 hour.

Place butter, water, salt, and sugar in a saucepan. When butter has melted, add peas. Cover and let simmer until very tender, about 10 minutes.

Drain and puree peas with cream in electric blender or force through a fine sieve.

NOTE: Recipe may be made ahead to this point.
Stir in lettuce.
Reheat just before serving. Correct seasoning with additional salt if needed.

○

MINTED PEAR HALVES

2 cups water
2 cups sugar
2 thin slices lemon
1 teaspoon mint-flavored extract
2 to 3 drops green food coloring
8 medium-size fresh pears

Place water, sugar, and lemon slices in a nonmetal saucepan over moderate heat. Stir until sugar has dissolved, then let syrup simmer while preparing pears.

Cut pears in half lengthwise. Peel each half, and with a small sharp spoon scoop out seeds and core. Add each pear half to syrup as soon as it is prepared.

Let the pears poach in the syrup until they are just tender. *Do not overcook*. Remove pan from heat and stir in the mint extract and food coloring. Let the pears cool in the syrup. Drain and serve at room temperature.

⊙

FRESH STRAWBERRY TARTS

2 *pints strawberries*
1 *package (8 ounces) cream cheese*
½ *cup light cream*
2 *tablespoons confectioners sugar*
8 *baked tart shells*
1 *jar (6 ounces) currant jelly*

You will need 4 or 5 medium-size strawberries for each tart. Hull and wash strawberries. Drain in colander.

Bring cream cheese to room temperature, then place it in a mixing bowl. Add cream and whip mixture until light and fluffy. Fold in sugar.

Cover the bottom of each tart shell with mixture, then fill with strawberries.

In a saucepan, melt jelly over low heat. Cool slightly, then spoon over strawberries to glaze.

Refrigerate tarts until about 1 hour before serving.

⊙

CARD-TABLE DINNER #4
(SERVES EIGHT)

Cold Green Beans with Curry Mayonnaise

Grilled Lamb Kebobs à la Turke

Persian Rice

Apricot Mousse

Coffee

Imported Philippine Beer

ALTERNATE: *Mexican Beer*

With this menu, omit wine. It tastes better when beer is served.

⊙

COLD GREEN BEANS
WITH CURRY MAYONNAISE

2 pounds fresh string beans
3 tablespoons lemon juice
3 tablespoons safflower or peanut oil
1 teaspoon sugar
½ teaspoon salt
½ teaspoon white pepper
2 tablespoons finely minced chives or parsley

Bring 3- or 4-quart pot of water to a rolling boil; wash beans and snap off string ends. Place beans in boiling water and boil briskly for 10 to 15 minutes—but check them as they cook the only way a good cook can: Take one out and try it! The beans should have lost all the "raw" taste but still retain a hint of crispness. As soon as the beans are done, drain them immediately and fill the pot with cold water, adding a few ice cubes if you wish. The idea is to stop the cooking at once. Done in this manner string beans have a wonderful just-picked flavor and retain their bright-green color. Drain the beans well and place them in a large non-metal bowl. Combine lemon juice, oil, sugar, salt, and pepper in a separate bowl. Blend mixture well and pour over beans. Refrigerate, covered, until ready to serve. Drain. Arrange on individual plates and garnish with curried mayonnaise (recipe below) and chives or parsley.

CURRIED MAYONNAISE
1 teaspoon curry powder
½ tablespoon lemon juice
1 cup homemade mayonnaise (recipe below)

Blend curry powder with lemon juice, stir into mayonnaise, and mix thoroughly. Refrigerate until ready to use.

MAYONNAISE

Homemade mayonnaise is so infinitely superior to the commercial variety it is a wonder that anyone will buy the latter. Especially when mayonnaise is so easy to make and—nice bonus—half the price of the store-bought variety. Successful mayonnaise is an emulsion that takes place when oil is slowly beaten into egg yolks combined with a small amount of acid liquid—vinegar or lemon juice—or a combination of both. The proportions are always the same: for each egg yolk, 1/2 cup of oil, 2 tablespoons of lemon juice and/or vinegar, and 1/4 teaspoon confectioners sugar. It's how they are combined that counts.

First, all ingredients must be slightly warm. If the room is a warm one, room temperature is suitable; if not, separate the yolks into a small bowl, measure out the oil, and place ingredients in a warm spot (near the oven perhaps) until every vestige of cold has disappeared. If you're not sure of the temperature, place the bowl of egg yolks in a larger bowl of warm water before starting.

Now combine your ingredients. The idea is to get your emulsion started—once it begins to thicken, you can relax.

To the egg yolks add 1/4 of the amount of the vinegar and the sugar. Beat well to blend and slowly add 1/2 of the total amount of the oil, drop by drop, beating constantly. It should start to thicken by now. Next add the remaining vinegar or lemon juice, a drop at a time, alternating with the remaining oil. It will be fluffy, thick, and delicious. Just be careful to add the oil very, very slowly. If you should make a mistake, all is not lost. Beat an extra yolk in a separate bowl and very slowly beat in the separated mayonnaise.

Seasoning is a matter of taste but the classic proportions are, to 1 egg yolk add 1/2 cup of oil, 1/4 teaspoon dry mustard, 1/4 teaspoon salt, few grains of cayenne pepper.

NOTE: Don't try to make mayonnaise during a thunderstorm. For some reason, it simply will not emulsify.

For quick reference, here are proportions:

2 tablespoons lemon juice and
2 tablespoons vinegar, mixed together
1/2 teaspoon salt
1/2 teaspoon confectioners sugar
Dash of cayenne pepper
2 egg yolks
1 cup salad oil

Combine 1/2 tablespoon of lemon juice, vinegar, salt, sugar, pepper, and egg yolks in a small bowl. Beat until blended. Add 1/2 cup of salad oil, drop by drop, beating constantly. When mayonnaise has started to thicken, add remaining salad oil and vinegar mixture alternately, again drop by drop, beating constantly. Beat until thick and fluffy. May be kept refrigerated and well covered, up to 1 week but no longer, so make mayonnaise as you use it.

Makes about 1½ cups of mayonnaise.

NOTE: A wire whisk will give you fluffier mayonnaise than a rotary beater.

⊙

GRILLED LAMB KEBOBS À LA TURKE

This professional chef's recipe may be prepared ahead and refrigerated until about an hour before serving time. The kebobs require only a few minutes' cooking time, but be careful to bring them to room temperature before broiling. If this is not done, they will be stone-cold inside.

> 2 pounds loin of lamb, cubed
> 1 cup canned pineapple juice
> ½ cup soy sauce
> 1 clove garlic, peeled and crushed
> ½ cup safflower or corn oil
> 4 tablespoons butter
> 32 large mushroom caps
> 16 slices bacon
> 16 fresh mint leaves
> ½ cup (1 stick) butter, melted
> 1 cup very fine dry bread crumbs
> Paprika

Have your butcher cut the lamb into cubes about ½ inch thick and 1¼ inches in diameter.

Combine pineapple juice, soy sauce, and garlic in a nonmetal bowl. Add lamb cubes and marinate for about 2 hours.

Drain meat and pat thoroughly dry with paper toweling.

In a heavy skillet, heat the oil to smoking and brown the lamb cubes a few at a time. Don't overcook. Remove each cube as soon as it is lightly browned. Set aside. Don't pierce the meat with a fork or juices and flavor will be lost.

When all meat has been browned, remove the oil from the pan and add the 4 tablespoons of butter. When butter has melted, add the mushrooms and sauté briefly, about 5 minutes. Set mushrooms aside.

Pour butter from pan and wipe pan clean with paper toweling. Add bacon to pan and cook over moderate heat until almost, but not quite, crisp.

Fill sixteen skewers with the lamb cubes, mushroom caps, bacon, and mint leaves—beginning and ending with mushroom caps and placing mint leaves next to the meat.

Preheat broiler.

Using a pastry brush, brush each kebob with melted butter, then roll in bread crumbs.

Place kebobs on broiler rack about 4 inches under heat and brown them briefly on all sides. Turn kebobs often, basting them with melted butter each time they are turned. Sprinkle with paprika.

Serve (two kebobs for each serving) over Persian Rice (recipe below).

⊙

PERSIAN RICE

2 tablespoons safflower or corn oil
2 small white onions, peeled and chopped
2 cups long-grained rice
3½ cups hot water
1½ teaspoons salt
½ cup raisins
½ cup chopped almonds
8 pitted dates, chopped

Heat the oil in a large, heavy saucepan. Add the onions and cook, stirring frequently, until they are soft but not browned, about 5 minutes. Add the rice and stir until each grain is coated with oil. Turn heat to very high and add water. Stir once, then bring to a full boil. Cover and immediately turn heat to very low. Let simmer for about 20 minutes or until tender. All liquid should have been absorbed by the rice; if not, drain.

Fluff the rice with a fork and gently fold in the raisins, almonds, and dates. Cover mixture and place in a preheated 200° F. oven for 10 minutes before serving.

○

APRICOT MOUSSE

1 pound dried apricots
1 cup sugar
2 tablespoons light white rum
2 cups heavy cream
4 crisp chocolate wafer cookies (commercially made)

Place apricots in a heavy enamelized cast-iron or other non-metal saucepan and add water to cover. Let soak several hours. Place pan over moderate heat. Add the sugar and let apricots simmer for about 25 minutes or until they are quite tender.

Drain off the cooking liquid and puree the apricots in an electric blender or force through a sieve. Place pureed apricots in a mixing bowl and stir in the rum. Refrigerate mixture until ready to use.

Chill the bowl and beater that you are going to use to whip the cream. Take cream from refrigerator and place in freezer for 15 minutes before whipping.

Whip cream until stiff, then fold it into the apricot puree.

Pour the mousse into small dessert dishes or, if you have them, porcelain petits pots, and refrigerate until well chilled. Crush cookies by placing them in a plastic bag and rolling it with a rolling pin. Sprinkle cookie crumbs on top of mousse.

TRICKS OF THE TRADE: The nearly frozen cream whips up in double-quick time in a chilled bowl and with a chilled beater.

⊙

CARD-TABLE DINNER #5
(SERVES EIGHT)

Scandinavian Cucumbers

Roast Loin of Pork with Sweet-Sour Glaze

Baked Stuffed Zucchini

Whipped Sweet Potatoes

Gingered Applesauce in Orange Shells

Pot du Crème au Chocolat

Coffee

WINE: *Bordeaux St. Julien*

⊙

SCANDINAVIAN CUCUMBERS

1 cup white wine vinegar
4 tablespoons sugar
¼ teaspoon salt
¼ teaspoon white pepper
3 tablespoons minced fresh dill
6 medium cucumbers
2 teaspoons freshly grated horseradish
1 cup sour cream
2 tablespoons capers
Watercress sprigs for garnish

Combine vinegar, sugar, salt, pepper, and dill in a large non-metal bowl. Wash cucumbers thoroughly (if waxed, scrub in very hot water); cut off ends but do not peel. Slice cucumbers as thinly as possible into even circles, then place them in the vinegar mixture. Cover and refrigerate for at least 3 hours or until ready to serve. Drain and arrange cucumbers on a serving plate. Mix horseradish and sour cream and top each serving with a small mound of the mixture. Sprinkle with capers and garnish with watercress.

⊙

ROAST LOIN OF PORK
WITH SWEET-SOUR GLAZE

1 three and a half- to four-pound loin of pork (8 ribs)
1 teaspoon salt
1 teaspoon pepper
1 cup wine vinegar
2 cups brown sugar
1 can (8 ounces) pineapple juice
2 tablespoons lemon rind
½ cup currant jelly
1 tablespoon soy sauce

Bring meat to room temperature before beginning. This is very important as meat will not cook properly if placed in the oven cold. Preheat oven to 450° F. Rub roast with salt and pepper and place on a rack in hot oven. Cook 15 to 20 minutes, then lower heat to 300° F. and cook 25 minutes to the pound or until a meat thermometer inserted in the roast reaches 190° F.

While the meat is cooking, combine all remaining ingredients except soy sauce in saucepan, heat to boiling, and stir until sugar is thoroughly dissolved. Baste meat two or three times while roasting.

When roast is done, remove it from oven and allow it to stand for at least 30 minutes before slicing. Add 1 tablespoon of the drippings in the roasting pan to the remaining glaze mixture and bring again to a boil. Remove pan from heat and stir in soy sauce. Baste roast four or five times with glaze while cooling. The more often you baste, the better it will taste. Use all the glaze for best results.

Carve meat into 8 serving slices and place on entrée platter.

○

BAKED STUFFED ZUCCHINI

4 medium-size zucchini
2 tablespoons butter
*3 tablespoons minced shallots or green onions (white part
    only)*
1 tablespoon tomato paste
½ teaspoon salt
½ teaspoon freshly ground black pepper
1 teaspoon dried oregano
½ teaspoon dried rosemary (optional)
½ cup fresh bread crumbs
¼ cup melted butter

Preheat oven to 350° F.

Wash zucchini and cut in half. With a teaspoon, scoop out
as much pulp as possible, taking care not to puncture the skins.
Chop pulp into small dice. Set aside.

Place zucchini shells in a shallow baking dish, cover tightly
with foil, and bake for 15 to 20 minutes until shells are tender but
not limp.

Melt the 2 tablespoons of butter in a small saucepan. Sauté
shallots in butter over low heat until limp but not brown. Add
zucchini pulp and remaining ingredients except bread crumbs
and continue to cook over low heat until pulp has softened and
mixture is well blended.

Remove mixture from heat. Stir in bread crumbs and stuff
zucchini shells. Brush with melted butter.

NOTE: At this point the stuffed shells may be refrigerated until
about 1 hour before serving.

When ready to continue, bring stuffed zucchini to room temperature and bake for 10 to 15 minutes in a 400° F. oven until
lightly browned.

⊙

WHIPPED SWEET POTATOES

4 medium-size sweet potatoes
¼ cup heavy cream
1 tablespoon butter, at room temperature
2 tablespoons orange juice
1 tablespoon grated orange rind
½ teaspoon salt

Preheat oven to 400° F.

Select similar-size potatoes that are free from blemish. Wash well and prick each potato a few times with a fork. Bake in preheated oven 30 to 45 minutes or until potatoes are soft. Remove from heat and allow to cool slightly.

Slit potatoes in half and scoop out pulp into a large mixing bowl. Add remaining ingredients to bowl. Beat mixture well with a heavy spoon until light and fluffy. Pile in shells.

NOTE: At this point potatoes may be refrigerated until about 1 hour before serving.

When ready to serve, bring potatoes to room temperature and bake in a preheated 300° F. oven until thoroughly heated, about 30 minutes.

⊙

GINGERED APPLESAUCE
IN ORANGE SHELLS

10 small tart apples
½ cup sugar
2 tablespoons butter
2 tablespoons finely chopped candied ginger
2 teaspoons grated lemon rind
8 orange shells

Peel and core the apples, then chop them into very small dice. Place diced apples in a nonmetal saucepan, one with a tight-fitting lid. Add sugar, butter, and about 2 tablespoons of water. Cover and cook over medium heat to a thick sauce, stirring occasionally.

Remove applesauce from heat. Stir in ginger and lemon rind. Refrigerate until ready to pile into orange shells.

⊙

POT DU CRÈME AU CHOCOLAT

This is a very easy, never-fail version of the classic chocolate custard.

¾ cup sugar
4 tablespoons flour
¼ teaspoon salt
4 egg yolks
3 cups milk
1 tablespoon butter
3 squares unsweetened chocolate
2 tablespoons cognac or 1 teaspoon vanilla

Combine sugar, flour, and salt in mixing bowl. Add eggs and stir until blended. Add 1 cup of the milk and beat with a wire whisk until smooth.

Transfer mixture to the top of a double boiler. Add remaining ingredients. Cook, stirring constantly, over simmering water until chocolate and butter are melted. Beat with a wire whisk until mixture is thick and smooth. If the custard becomes lumpy while cooking, remove it from the heat and stir, mashing the lumps smooth against the side of the pot. Then use your whisk to re-blend. Cook until custard is as thick as heavy cream. Pour, hot, into pot du crème pots, and chill well before serving.

Serves 8 with a bit left over for "tomorrow."

⊙

CARD-TABLE DINNER #6
(SERVES EIGHT)

Cold Stuffed Beets on Bibb or Boston Lettuce Leaves

Vitello Tonnato

Hot Crusty Italian Rolls

Fruit à l'Angleterre

Crisp Walnut Cookies

Coffee

WINE: *Chilled Soave (Italian White Wine)*

This dinner menu is especially good in hot weather.

⊙

COLD STUFFED BEETS ON LETTUCE LEAVES

2 cans (no. 2) whole baby beets
2 cups white wine vinegar
2 tablespoons sugar
1 small white onion, peeled and sliced
8 water chestnuts, drained and chopped
2 stalks celery, chopped
2 tablespoons chopped, preserved ginger
2 tablespoons lemon juice
1 teaspoon Chinese dry mustard
1 cup mayonnaise (see page 71)
Crisp lettuce leaves

Drain canned beets and place in a nonmetal saucepan. Add vinegar, sugar, and onion. Bring mixture to a full boil, lower heat, and let simmer for 5 minutes. Remove from heat. Cool slightly, then refrigerate, covered, until well chilled or until ready to proceed with recipe.

To prepare the beets for stuffing, drain them well and cut

out the center of each with a small sharp knife. Then use a spoon to shape and scrape the insides of the beets into smooth hollow bowls.

Chop the scooped-out beet centers and combine them with the chopped water chestnuts, celery, and ginger.

Mix together the lemon juice and dry mustard until smooth. Stir this into the mayonnaise. Add ½ of the seasoned mayonnaise to the chopped vegetables. Stuff beets with mixture.

For each serving, arrange 3 or 4 beets on a lettuce leaf on small appetizer or salad plate and top each with a little of the remaining mayonnaise.

⊙

VITELLO TONNATO
(COLD VEAL SLICES WITH TUNA FISH SAUCE)

THE VEAL

3 pounds boneless veal in one piece
1 clove garlic, peeled and cut into slivers
Water, as needed
1½ cups dry white wine
1 veal knuckle bone, cut up
1 carrot, scraped and cut up
2 medium-size onions, peeled and each stuck with 1 clove
2 stalks celery with leaves, cut up
4 sprigs parsley
1 teaspoon salt
½ teaspoon thyme
10 whole peppercorns
2 whole bay leaves

THE SAUCE

½ cup olive oil
1 egg yolk
1 small can (4 ounces) Italian tuna fish in olive oil
5 anchovy fillets, cut up
½ cup mayonnaise, preferably homemade (page 71)
2 tablespoons lemon juice
¼ cup veal stock
2 tablespoons capers

GARNISH

1 tomato, peeled, seeded and sliced
1 hard-cooked egg, sliced
2 lemons, quartered
16 pitted black olives
2 tablespoons minced parsley
1 tablespoon minced green onions (green part only)

TO COOK THE VEAL: Have your butcher remove all skin and fat and tie the meat securely.

Make small incisions along the entire length of the meat with a small sharp knife. Insert a sliver of garlic deep into each incision.

Place meat in a large heavy pot, preferably an enamelized cast-iron one. Add sufficient water to cover, bring to a full boil, and skim surface until completely clear. Lower heat. Add wine, veal knuckle, vegetables, and seasoning. Partially cover pot and let simmer until meat is tender, about 2 hours. Remove pot from heat and let meat cool to room temperature in the stock.

Remove meat and set aside. Skim fat from stock and strain it into a second pan. Add meat and refrigerate until ready to prepare sauce.

TO PREPARE SAUCE: Place olive oil, egg yolk, tuna fish, and anchovies in electric blender and blend to a smooth paste. Transfer this mixture to a small bowl and stir in the mayonnaise, lemon juice, veal stock, and capers. Blend well. (If you do not have an electric blender, you can prepare this by hand: Mince fine the tuna fish and anchovies and force through a fine sieve into the mixing bowl. Beat in olive oil, then add remaining ingredients, blending well after each addition.)

TO ASSEMBLE DISH: Take cool meat from stock and with a sharp knife cut it into thin, even slices.

Spread the bottom of a large, shallow, oblong glass (or other nonmetal) platter with a thin layer of the sauce. Cover this with the veal slices in a single layer and pour the rest of the sauce over them.

Cover veal platter securely with plastic wrap or foil. This is important as prolonged exposure to air will discolor your creamy white sauce. Refrigerate veal slices 4 or more hours so that the sauce will penetrate and flavor the meat. Remove the platter from the refrigerator about 2 hours before serving, but do not uncover the veal until just a short time before the dish is to be brought to the table.

Garnish meat platter with tomato slices, slices of hard-cooked egg, lemon wedges, and olives. Sprinkle parsley and green onions over sauce and serve at room temperature.

NOTE: Don't discard the leftover veal stock. It's great to have on hand. Just cover it and refrigerate. It will congeal into a rich jelly. Remove and discard all additional fat that has come to the surface and use stock instead of water when preparing any soup or stew. Stock will keep 2 to 3 weeks in the refrigerator if it is covered and sealed from air with plastic wrap and if it is reheated to full rolling boil and boiled for a full 3 minutes every 5 to 6 days; it is imperative to follow this procedure so that the stock does not spoil and cause food poisoning. It can also be wrapped securely and sealed, then frozen for as long as two or three months.

⊙

FRUIT À L'ANGLETERRE

> *1 cup sugar*
> *½ cup water*
> *½ cup orange juice*
> *2 tablespoons grated orange peel*
> *16 small peaches*
> *3 tablespoons Grand Marnier or Cointreau liqueur (optional)*
> *1 cup green grapes*
> *4 large oranges*
> *1 large cantaloupe*

In a saucepan combine sugar, water, and orange juice and peel. Bring to a full boil, then lower heat and let simmer for 5 minutes.

Plunge peaches into boiling water for a moment, then into cold water. Slip off skins. Cut peaches in half and remove stones. Place peaches in orange syrup and let simmer for 10 to 15 minutes or until tender. Remove from heat and add liqueur and grapes.

While this is cooling, peel and section oranges, removing all white pith and seeds (an easy task if your knife is razor sharp). Peel and cut cantaloupe into balls or small chunks.

Add to fruit in syrup. Cover and chill. Serve icy cold.

⊙

CRISP WALNUT COOKIES

1 cup butter at room temperature
¾ cup sugar
2 eggs well beaten
1¾ cups flour
1 teaspoon vanilla
¼ cup honey at room temperature
1 cup finely chopped walnuts

Preheat oven to 375° F.

Cream the butter until light and fluffy. Add the sugar a little at a time and beat after each addition. Add the eggs and blend well. Fold in the flour and vanilla.

Add honey to walnuts and mix well.

Drop batter from the tip of a teaspoon to a greased baking sheet. Spread each cookie thin with a knife that has first been dipped in cold water. Sprinkle with the chopped walnuts. Bake in preheated 375° F. oven for 8 to 10 minutes. They should be lightly browned, thin and crisp.

Makes about 5 dozen cookies.

NOTE: Store in air tight container. Will stay fresh for 10 days to two weeks.

⊙

CARD-TABLE DINNER #7
(SERVES EIGHT)

Cold Salmon Timbales

Watercress Garnish

Sautéed Boned Breast of Chicken

Kasha with Peas

Corn-stuffed Tomatoes

Peach Cream

Coffee

WINE: *Lightly Chilled Puligny-Montrachet*
ALTERNATE: *Italian Soave*

○

COLD SALMON TIMBALES

This delicious cold salmon is well worth the doing—and while we
have planned for individual molds for our dinner party, the same
recipe may be used in a fish-shaped mold for a spectacular buffet
dish, especially on a warm summer night. Needless to say, these
timbales can be made the day before the party.

Bones and head of 1 large salmon
1 carrot, sliced
1 small onion, peeled and quartered
1 bay leaf
1 cup dry white wine
2 pounds salmon, free of skin and bones
2 envelopes unflavored gelatin
¼ pound butter, at room temperature
1 egg white
½ teaspoon salt
¼ teaspoon white pepper
¼ cup boiling water or fish stock
½ cup heavy cream
1 cup homemade mayonnaise (page 71)
16 pimento-stuffed olives, thinly sliced

Place salmon bones and head in a large heavy pot. Cover with
cold water, add carrots, onion, bay leaf, and wine. Bring mixture
to a boil, then lower to simmer. Wrap salmon carefully in an
oblong piece of clean cheesecloth, making sure the ends of the cloth
are long enough to hang over the sides of the pot so the fish may
be removed easily. Poach salmon in the gently simmering liquid
for 12 to 15 minutes, then lift from stock to a large platter and
allow to cool slightly before unwrapping. Strain stock, discarding
head, bones, and vegetables. Bring the liquid to a boil and cook
rapidly until amount is reduced to about 1½ cups. Soften 1 envelope of the gelatin in a small amount of cold water and dissolve
it in hot stock. Pour about 1 inch of gelatin mixture in the bottom

of 8 individual timbale molds that have been lightly greased with salad oil. Place molds in refrigerator to set.

Force salmon meat through the finest blade of a food chopper twice. Add the softened butter to the fish and blend well. Blend in egg white. Force mixture through food chopper again. Place mixture in a large bowl set in a pan of cracked ice or ice cubes and beat with a wooden spoon until light and airy. Soften remaining envelope of gelatin in cold water, then dissolve it in boiling water or stock if there is enough remaining. Blend gelatin into salmon mixture. Whip the cream until stiff and fold it into the salmon. (If stock in timbale molds has not yet set, place salmon mixture in refrigerator briefly, but not long enough for it to set.) Pour salmon over jellied stock in molds and refrigerate, covered with foil. When ready to serve, dip molds briefly into hot water and run a wet knife around the edge. Timbales will slip out easily onto the plate. Garnish each plate with homemade mayonnaise and sliced olives.

○

SAUTÉED BONED BREAST OF CHICKEN

8 chicken breasts, boned
1 cup flour
1 teaspoon salt
1 teaspoon freshly ground black pepper
1 teaspoon dried marjoram, crumbled
½ cup safflower or peanut oil
½ cup sweet butter
¼ cup cognac
16 mushroom caps
½ cup dry white wine
½ cup fresh or canned chicken stock

Flatten the chicken breasts slightly with a wooden mallet. Combine flour, salt, pepper, and marjoram. Dip chicken pieces into flour mixture, making sure that they are well but not heavily coated.

Heat oil and butter in a deep, heavy sauté pan, one with a lid, and brown the chicken pieces, a few pieces at a time. When the chicken takes on a light color remove to a heated platter and keep hot. When all pieces are browned, pour off all but about 3 tablespoons of the oil and butter. Return the chicken pieces to the pan, cover, and cook over very low heat 10 to 15 minutes, shaking the pan occasionally.

Remove pan from heat and let stand, covered, for an additional 10 minutes. Heat the cognac and return pan to low heat. Uncover pan and pour the cognac over the chicken; ignite and let flame die out.

Transfer chicken to an ovenproof dish. Add mushroom caps, wine, and stock to pan. Cook over medium heat until mushrooms are tender.

Transfer mushrooms to chicken dish, pour sauce over chicken, cover, and keep in low oven (about 250° F.) until ready to serve.

⊙

KASHA WITH PEAS

3 tablespoons butter
1½ cups kasha
2 cups chicken stock
2 cups water
1 teaspoon salt
2 packages (10 ounces) frozen green peas
2 tablespoons minced parsley

Melt butter in a deep, heavy saucepan. Add kasha and cook over low heat until each grain is evenly coated. Add stock, water, and salt. Cook over low heat for 40 to 45 minutes.

Defrost peas by plunging briefly into hot water and draining them. Stir peas into Kasha. Keep hot over boiling water until ready to serve.

Immediately before serving, sprinkle with chopped parsley.

⊙

CORN-STUFFED TOMATOES

3 tablespoons butter
2 tablespoons minced shallots or green onions
8 medium-size firm tomatoes
½ teaspoon salt
½ teaspoon pepper
½ teaspoon dried thyme
½ teaspoon sugar
1 package (10 ounces) frozen kernel corn
4 tablespoons fresh bread crumbs

Preheat oven to 400° F.

Melt the butter in a heavy skillet and sauté the minced shallots or green onions just until soft; do not allow them to brown. Cut the tops off the tomatoes and squeeze them gently to remove seeds. Scoop out tomato pulp and add it to sautéed shallots. Sprinkle tomatoes shells with salt and place them upside down to drain. Add pepper, thyme, sugar, and corn (which need not be defrosted) to shallot-tomato mixture and cook briefly over medium heat until corn is thoroughly hot. Blend in bread crumbs. Stuff tomato shells with mixture, place them in a buttered baking dish, and bake for about 15 minutes or until shells are just tender. Do not overcook.

NOTE: Tomatoes may be stuffed and refrigerated until 30 to 45 minutes before needed. Bring them to room temperature before baking as directed.

⊙

PEACH CREAM

1 package (10 ounces) frozen peaches
3 envelopes unflavored gelatin
½ cup boiling water
½ cup orange juice
1 tablespoon cognac (optional)
1 quart vanilla ice cream
¾ cup macaroon crumbs
2 cups heavy cream

Defrost peaches until they separate easily. Soften gelatin in a little cold water, add boiling water, and stir to dissolve thoroughly. Add orange juice and cognac.

Place ice cream in large mixing bowl and soften slightly by beating for a moment. Add partially thawed peaches, gelatin mixture, and macaroon crumbs. Blend. Place mixture in refrigerator.

Whip the cream until very stiff, then fold it into ice cream-peach mixture. Pour into a 6-cup soufflé mold and refrigerate until set.

NOTE: Use the best-quality French ice cream available. The cheaper variety contains less butterfat and will not soften, but only becomes liquid. Strawberries or bananas may be substituted if peaches are unavailable. Sprinkle the cut bananas with lemon juice to avoid darkening.

⊙

CARD-TABLE DINNER #8
(SERVES EIGHT)

Jellied Tomato Consommé with Cucumber and Fresh Dill
Cold Glazed Corned Brisket of Beef
Steamed New Potatoes
Steamed Green Cabbage
Honey-glazed Onions
Hot Deep-dish Peach Pie
Coffee
Irish Beer or Pale Ale

This menu is a summer favorite.

⊙

JELLIED TOMATO CONSOMMÉ
WITH CUCUMBER AND FRESH DILL

4 large tomatoes
3 cups fresh or canned chicken stock
1 teaspoon sugar
½ teaspoon salt
¼ teaspoon white pepper
Dash of nutmeg
2 envelopes unflavored gelatin
1 large or 2 small cucumbers
1 tablespoon fresh dill, minced
Sour cream (optional)

Quarter the tomatoes and combine them with stock, sugar, salt, pepper, and nutmeg. Cook over medium heat, stirring occasionally until tomatoes are very soft.

Soften gelatin in a small amount of cold water. Strain hot tomato-stock mixture into a large bowl through a very fine sieve lined with cheesecloth, pressing tomato pulp down firmly to extract juice. Discard pulp. Stir in softened gelatin and stir mixture until dissolved. Chill soup until firmly jellied.

Peel and dice cucumbers. Break up jellied soup with a fork, pile into chilled consommé cups, garnish with cucumbers and minced fresh dill. You can add a dollop of sour cream if you like.

⊙

COLD GLAZED CORNED BRISKET OF BEEF

4½- to 5-pound corned brisket of beef (first cut)
2 garlic cloves, peeled
2 small onions, each studded with 4 cloves
2 teaspoons mixed pickling spice
1 carrot, peeled and quartered
2 bay leaves
1 tablespoon sugar
¼ cup red wine vinegar
½ cup apricot jam
1 small can (6 ounces) preserved mandarin orange slices

Be sure to ask for first-cut brisket as it has less fat and is the easiest cut to slice. Place the brisket in a 5- or 6-quart nonmetal pot and cover with cold water. Add garlic, onions, pickling spice, carrot, bay leaves, sugar, and vinegar. Bring meat to a boil, then lower heat to simmer and cook slowly for approximately 3 hours or until tender but not falling apart. Remove pot from heat and allow brisket to cool in broth for 30 minutes. Remove brisket from broth and place meat in a shallow storage dish; cover with foil, and refrigerate until well chilled.

Melt the apricot jam with two tablespoons of the syrup from the orange sections. Allow mixture to cool to room temperature.

Slice the brisket into serving portions, then re-form to appear to be a solid piece of meat. Spread brisket evenly with glaze. Poach the orange sections in the remaining glaze, cool, and then garnish the brisket with the oranges.

○

STEAMED NEW POTATOES

24 small new potatoes, none more than 2 inches in diameter
3 tablespoons butter, at room temperature
1 cup water
1 teaspoon salt
2 tablespoons chopped parsley

Wash potatoes under cold running water and scrape off any damaged skin.

Place potatoes in a large, heavy frying pan—10 to 12 inches in diameter (use one with a tight-fitting lid). Add the butter and water to the pan. Cover and cook over low heat until potatoes are tender, about 20 minutes.

Shake pan often and check occasionally to make sure that the liquid has not completely boiled away, but uncover pan as little as possible. When vegetables are done, pour off cooking liquid and shake pan over heat until potatoes are dry.

Steamed potatoes are at their best served the minute they are done, but if they must wait, place them, uncovered, in a 250° F. oven for as long as 15 minutes *but no longer,* then reheat in hot melted butter. Sprinkle with salt and parsley immediately before serving.

⊙

STEAMED GREEN CABBAGE

1 large green cabbage
3 green onions, chopped
2 tablespoons butter, at room temperature
Salt
Freshly ground black pepper
1 tablespoon lemon juice
2 tablespoons water

Cut off loose outer leaves of cabbage and any bruised spots. Wash cabbage thoroughly and cut into eight wedges. Cut off thick part of core, leaving enough to hold wedges together. Wash each cabbage wedge under cold running water.

Place wedges with water clinging to them in a large 10- to 12-inch skillet. Add green onions and butter. Sprinkle with salt, pepper, lemon juice, and water. Cover cabbage wedges with outer leaves. Cover skillet and place over moderate heat. Let cabbage steam for 8 minutes. Check for doneness. Cabbage wedges should be tender but still slightly crisp. Continue to cook if necessary, but don't overcook.

This method of cooking results in a light and delicate vegetable that is completely unlike the heavy boiled cabbage mother (or was it grandmother?) used to prepare.

⊙

HONEY-GLAZED ONIONS

24 small white onions
4 tablespoons butter
4 tablespoons water
½ cup honey

Peel and trim onions. Melt butter over low heat in a saucepan that has a tight-fitting lid. Add onions and water. Cover tightly and cook over very low heat for about 20 minutes. Shake pan occasionally but do not uncover while cooking.

When onions are tender but not "mushy," add honey and cook slowly, stirring occasionally until onions are glazed. They can successfully be reheated over very low heat.

⊙

HOT DEEP-DISH PEACH PIE

5 cups fresh peaches, peeled and sliced
1 cup sugar
½ cup currant jelly
2 tablespoons quick-cooking tapioca
2 tablespoons cognac or brandy
2 tablespoons butter
Pastry for pie crust
1 egg white
Cream (optional)

Preheat oven to 400° F.

Combine peaches, sugar, currant jelly, tapioca, and cognac. Let mixture stand for 15 or 20 minutes. Fill baking dish with mixture and dot with butter. Roll out pastry and cover pie evenly, crimping with a fork to seal. Place pie in preheated oven. Immediately lower heat to 300° F. and bake for about 40 minutes. The crust should be crisply tender but not brown. Remove pie from heat and refrigerate until about 1 hour before serving.

Allow the pie to come to room temperature. Beat the egg white with a small amount of water and brush it over pie crust. Place the pie in a 250° F. oven for 30 minutes or until hot. Crust should be lightly browned.

Serve with heavy unsweetened cream or sour cream if desired.

Buffet Dinner Parties

⊙

Everybody knows that buffet dinners are the easiest of all parties to give. It is perfectly possible to have two dozen or more guests for a buffet and not require any outside help. All it takes is planning and a menu that can be prepared ahead, plus a few pieces of handy equipment.

YOUR GUESTS

Who should be invited to a buffet party? I usually start by asking a few close friends, then keep adding more until I have a crowd. At a buffet party you can mix and match people—bridge the generation gap—and get by with an uneven number of guests.

I start with two or three couples I like and who know one another, then ask their adult children and/or the couples' parents. I often add a marvelous new-to-the-neighborhood man I would like to know better. And then—why not?—the boss and his wife. With so many people gathered, they always will find someone to talk to. I also ask one or more unattached women. At this type of party there is no need to find a single man for each one.

INVITATIONS

Should you send out written invitations? I do. Telephone invitations are perfectly acceptable but written invitations some-how give any party more sparkle right from the start. Be specific, however; avoid such scribbled notes as "Come to the party" or "We are having a party Saturday night. Please come." Instead, state the time, place, and dress with something like this: "We are having a few friends in for an informal buffet supper from 7 to 10 on Saturday night the 30th. Won't you join us?"

PARTY STRATEGY

Once you have received answers to about three-fourths of your invitations, don't wait. It's time to map out your party strategy. First decide on your menu. Then write it down—and, starting with appetizers, check the equipment you have on hand against the food you're planning to prepare. Do you have sufficient large ovenproof casseroles? A good-size double boiler for reheating precooked food? Large mixing bowls, etc.? If not, now's the time

to buy, rent, or borrow as oversize cooking equipment is sometimes hard to find.

SERVING EQUIPMENT

Next check over your serving dishes. You may need more
plates than you have in one pattern. No matter—for all but the
most formal buffet tables you can use alternate stacks of two patterns, mix and match, or fill in with inexpensive plain white or
clear-glass plates.

For a really large party, you can rent what you need to fill in
the gaps. Rates for this sort of equipment are usually quite reasonable, and most caterers can supply you with everything you will
need from cocktail glasses to demitasse cups. You can, however,
find quite attractive flatware at reasonable prices in almost any
good department store, and plain glasses in every imaginable size
are to be had for less than it will cost you to rent them.

Hot dishes must be kept hot. For each one you are going to
serve you will need a candle-warmer stand or, even handier, an
electric hot tray that will hold two generous-size casseroles. I am
lucky enough to have inherited a handsome old-fashioned silver
serving dish with a lower compartment that can be filled with hot
water that keeps food hot without drying it out. Similar dishes
can be rented from a caterer.

You will also need platters, which can be silver, pottery, china,
or even pewter, depending on the mood of your room and your
style of living. It's usually more appealing to vary the shapes—
oval, round, and oblong. Bread and crackers are most attractive
in napkin-lined baskets that can be picked up at any number of
gift shops or even at your local five-and-ten. Lastly, the problem
of hot coffee has to be dealt with, and if this is to be an informal
gathering, the easiest solution is one of those handy, set-ahead,
stay-hot electric coffee makers. However, if the occasion calls for
a more formal look, a silver coffee urn with its own spirit lamp is
usually available from a caterer.

Now that the matter of equipment is out of the way, you can
go on to the actual buffet service.

TABLE SETTINGS

The best strategy for easy and gracious service is to have not
one but actually three buffets—a small side table for appetizer

service, a main table for the entrée dishes and wine service, and a dessert service table. They need not all be in the dining room. The dessert service can be in the hall or in the living room, or out on the terrace in mild weather.

First, the appetizer table . . . It's usually a good idea to have the appetizer already set out on individual plates. This tactic helps get the dinner under way with less confusion among the guests. The table should be set with small napkins to the left, next, the silver necessary for the course—usually only a fork—and a basket for crackers or toast if desired. You will need space for the individual plates so there's usually not much room for decorations. Let the food and a pretty cloth take their place.

Now for the main table setting . . . Again napkins go on the left-hand side of the table, folded and placed so that each napkin is overlapped by the next. Following to the right is the silver (the implements needed depend of course on the menu.) Plates come next and are in two or three stacks, never more than six plates to a stack. The main dishes are centered and the supporting cast—casseroles, breads, relishes, etc.—take up the right side of the table.

TABLE DECORATIONS

Buffet tables usually look prettiest with two decorative arrangements rather than a centerpiece, and here is where you can let the sky be the limit. Small topiary trees are easy and fun to make and can vary with the season and the mood. Take a narrow round stick and twine it with green florist's tape. Place the stick in a clay flowerpot that has been firmly packed with "Oasis" (a green substance that is used for flower arrangements). Moisten the Oasis to make it easy to pack into the pot. Place the stick upright in the Oasis and attach a round Styrofoam ball to the top of the stick. Now you can cover the ball in whatever suits your party mood—small red carnations and holly for Christmas, bachelor buttons and daisies, tiny rosebuds, ivy, gardenias, camelias, any fairly compact flower with a firm stem. If need be, the flowers can be wired onto small florist sticks to anchor them securely in the Styrofoam. All the above-mentioned supplies may be purchased at almost any florist or variety store.

Decorations are by no means limited to cut flowers. Try an arrangement of crystal animals or fruit on a deep green cloth set with gleaming silver, or simply tall candlesticks covered with glittering hurricane shades, or, for the fall harvest table, a pair of small pumpkins filled with sheaves of wheat. Among the most effective decorations are silver bowls filled with tiny boxes wrapped in glossy white paper and tied with silver ribbon. Every box contains a small favor for a guest. This is especially effective at Christmas when they can be flanked by gold and silver foil angels and tall candles in silver holders.

You can also create a very fresh-looking table with potted plants. Try a row of pink and red geraniums on a pink cloth, or spring bulbs can be color keyed to a cloth—purple hyacinth on olive green, daffodils on a pale yellow. Tulips, pots of violets, even tiny boxwood are all suitable for decorative effects. Be sure to keep them in their own natural clay pots—that's part of the charm.

Buffet tables should either be beautifully polished bare wood or covered with a floor-length cloth. Nothing looks worse than a buffet tablecloth with the conventional 12-inch or 14-inch drop, and party cloths are so easy to make in marvelous colors and patterns that there really is no excuse for a routine cloth. However, if your tables are beautiful in themselves, then simply polish, polish, polish, and use the prettiest big napkins you can find— anything from silky damasks to bright bandanas, depending on the look you want to create.

For your dessert table, it's fun to vary the colors or patterns, especially if this table is set up in another room. Naturally you must keep to a compatible color; for example, if your main tablecloth is green and decorated with daffodils or yellow tulips, a spigged yellow cloth might be very effective for the dessert table. But remember, when purchasing tablecloth material the best policy is to shop around for swatches of fabrics and bring them home to see how they look in your house and with your china before you commit yourself.

All full-length cloths require a liner; plain white flannel with a pinked hem is perfect and easy to make. You should have one for each table and place it under every cloth you use.

SEATING YOUR GUESTS

Once you have planned and assembled your equipment and mapped out your table arrangement, you should consider how people are going to be seated. Seating can be as elaborate as little tables set for four or six, each with its own centerpiece, silver, and bottle of wine, or as informal as a strategically arranged living room that allows each guest a spot for his plate where he can eat comfortably. If your living-room table decor simply does not lend itself to the latter, use little individual folding tables that can be set up quickly and whisked out of sight when dinner is over. Have them stacked either in or near the living room for quick access.

SERVING

This brings us up to the actual party. The food has been prepared, and the table set. The only thing left to do is to set up the bar. If the get-together is small and casual and guests are going to serve themselves, the bar can be any place that is convenient to get to without causing a traffic jam. If the gathering is large, you might consider hiring a bartender and set up a bar for him to work from in a second room, or, if it's a warm evening, outside on the terrace.

I limit cocktail time to one hour after the arrival of my first few guests. Then I announce dinner.

As all food has been prepared—hot food in serving dishes in the warming oven, cold food in bowls or on platters in the re-frigerator—all that remains to do is to place it on the buffet tables.

I usually help the first two or three guests serve their plates. For some reason no one ever seems to want to be the first to serve himself, but once they begin they enjoy it. A buffet table is fun—especially when the food is attractively presented. It's a great kind of party.

A final note about help . . . You don't need anyone to help serve the meal and you can easily get by without assistance of any kind, but it is a great comfort to have someone in the kitchen to help bring the food to the table, gather up empty cocktail glasses, empty ash trays two or three times during the evening, remove empty plates after the meal, and then, bless them to heaven, wash the dishes and clean up the kitchen.

⊙

INFORMAL WINTER BUFFET PARTY
FOR TWELVE

Cold Roast Turkey Platter with Cornbread Stuffing

Jellied Cranberry-Orange Relish

Hot Casserole of Creamed Sweetbreads, Oysters, and Ham

Toast Points

Southern Cold Cooked Vegetable Salad

Hot Buttered Rolls

Brandied Plum Cake

Louisiana Ambrosia

Sand Tarts

Espresso

WINE: *Dry California Champagne*

⊙

ROAST TURKEY
WITH CORNBREAD STUFFING

This recipe uses the old-fashioned high-temperature method of roasting which results in crispy delicious skin and juicy flavorful meat. It's wonderful buffet-party fare and almost no trouble to prepare when taken step by step. Prepare the stock, make the cornbread, prepare the stuffing, and roast the bird.

STOCK
Turkey liver and giblets
1 stalk celery with leaves
1 large white onion
2 sprigs parsley
½ teaspoon salt
6 peppercorns
1 bay leaf
8 cups water

Place all ingredients in a saucepan and bring to a full boil. Lower heat and let simmer for 2 to 3 hours. (Remove turkey liver as soon as tender.) Set aside.

Chop giblets and liver. Strain stock.

CORNBREAD
4 tablespoons butter
1½ cups yellow cornmeal
1 cup flour
½ teaspoon salt
1 tablespoon sugar
2 eggs
1 cup milk
1 tablespoon corn or safflower oil

Preheat oven to 375° F.

Melt the butter in an 8- or 9-inch cast-iron or enamelized cast-iron skillet.

Combine remaining ingredients in mixing bowl. Add melted butter and blend well.

Heat the oil in the skillet in which the butter was melted. When oil is very hot, pour in the cornbread mixture. Place immediately in the preheated oven and bake until firm, about 25 minutes. Cool, then crumble cornbread.

STUFFING
Boiled turkey giblets and liver, chopped
1 cup chopped pecans
Crumbled cornbread
½ cup finely chopped onion
½ cup finely chopped celery
4 tablespoons butter
2 eggs
2 cups turkey stock
Salt
Pepper

Place chopped giblets and liver in a large mixing bowl. Add chopped pecans and crumbled cornbread.

Sauté onions and celery in butter until soft. Add to cornbread mixture. Add eggs and stock. Blend well and season to taste with salt and pepper.

ROAST TURKEY
1 ten- to twelve-pound turkey
Stuffing (recipe above)
¼ pound butter, softened
Salt

Preheat oven to 450° F.

Stuff and truss turkey. Don't overstuff. (Reserve remaining stuffing to be baked separately.)

Spread surface of bird with soft butter. Sprinkle with salt.

Place turkey in a large roasting pan, breast side up, and roast for 15 minutes. Turn bird breast side down and roast for 15 minutes longer. Reduce oven temperature to 350° F. and continue to roast, basting the turkey often with fat from the pan and spreading occasionally with soft butter. If skin becomes too brown, cover the bird loosely with aluminum foil.

Roast turkey 30 minutes to the pound.

TO SERVE HOT: Untruss turkey and let stand for about 20 minutes before carving.

TO SERVE COLD: Cool bird to room temperature, then wrap securely and refrigerate until about 1 hour before carving. Bring turkey to room temperature, then carve. Arrange turkey on platter, alternating slices of turkey with slices of cornbread stuffing.

TO BAKE STUFFING NOT USED IN TURKEY: Spoon into a breadloaf pan and place in preheated 375° F. oven and bake until firm, about 30 minutes. Serve stuffing hot or refrigerate, covered, in baking pan. Turn out when cold and cut into thin slices.

⊙

JELLIED CRANBERRY-ORANGE RELISH

3 cups raw cranberries
1 large orange
1 package cherry Jell-O
1 cup hot water
1 cup sugar
1 tablespoon (1 envelope) unflavored gelatin
1 cup orange juice
½ cup finely chopped walnuts
1 tablespoon prepared horseradish
Lettuce leaves

Wash cranberries under cold water. Pat dry with paper toweling. Quarter orange and remove seeds. Put cranberries and orange through medium blade of meat grinder.

Dissolve Jell-O in hot water. Add sugar.

Dissolve plain gelatin in orange juice in top of double boiler over, *not in,* simmering water. Combine gelatin mixtures. Chill until partially set. Add ground cranberries-orange mixture and walnuts. Stir in horseradish.

Pour mixture into 12 individual molds and chill until firm. Unmold onto small lettuce leaves.

NOTE: Grease molds lightly with mayonnaise before pouring in the relish and they will slip out easily when unmolded.

⊙

HOT CASSEROLE OF CREAMED SWEETBREADS, OYSTERS, AND HAM

2 pairs sweetbreads
2 tablespoons lemon juice
1 teaspoon salt
2 tablespoons minced shallots
4 tablespoons flour
4 tablespoons butter
2½ cups milk
¼ cup dry vermouth
½ cup liquid from oysters
Pepper
Salt
36 small oysters, drained
2 cups diced cooked lean ham, preferably baked Virginia ham
½ cup fine dry bread crumbs
2 tablespoons melted butter

Soak the sweetbreads in ice water for one hour. Drain. Place in a large saucepan and add boiling water to cover. Add lemon juice and salt. Let simmer for 15 minutes. Remove sweetbreads from water with a slotted spoon and immediately place them in a pan of ice water. Drain again. Break into small pieces, removing all membranes, connective tissues, and tubes. Set sweetbreads aside.

In a large saucepan, sauté the shallots in the butter until soft. Stir in the flour and cook, stirring, over low heat for 2 to 3 minutes. Slowly add the milk, stirring as it is added. Add the vermouth and continue to cook, stirring almost constantly until the sauce thickens. Add oyster liquid and season lightly with salt and pepper.

Add sweetbreads, oysters, and ham. Continue to cook for 5 minutes. Taste and correct seasoning with additional salt if needed.

Spoon the mixture into a buttered ovenproof casserole. Sprinkle with bread crumbs and moisten with melted butter.

NOTE: Recipe can be made ahead to this point. Cover casserole and let stand at room temperature for no more than one hour before proceeding—or cover and refrigerate until one hour before proceeding.

Place casserole in a preheated 375° F. oven and bake for 10 minutes or until crumb topping is lightly browned.

⊙

SOUTHERN COLD COOKED VEGETABLE SALAD

1 cup cooked diced carrots
1 cup cooked diced green beans
1 cup cooked peas
1 cup cooked lima beans
1 cup chopped celery
2 tablespoons finely minced green pepper
1 tablespoon finely minced parsley
2 tablespoons finely minced sweet pickles
1 tablespoon finely minced chives
1 tablespoon finely minced capers
1 cup French dressing
Lettuce leaves
1 cup cooked cauliflower flowerettes
½ cup mayonnaise (page 71)
2 tablespoons chopped pimento
Black and green olives

The carrots, green beans, peas, and lima beans used may be either canned or fresh. All vegetables should be cooked separately only until barely tender.

In a large bowl combine carrots, green beans, peas, lima beans, and celery. Add green pepper, parsley, sweet pickles, chives, capers, and French dressing. Toss to blend. Cover and refrigerate 2 hours or longer.

NOTE: Recipe can be made ahead to this point.

Drain vegetables. Line salad bowl with lettuce leaves and fill with drained vegetables.

Mix cauliflower flowerettes and pimento with mayonnaise. Top the mound of vegetables with the cauliflower mixture. Garnish the bowl with black and green olives.

⊙

BRANDIED PLUM CAKE

½ teaspoon salt
¼ teaspoon nutmeg
1½ cups flour
½ cup seeded raisins
½ cup currants
½ cup finely diced citron
½ cup finely diced candied orange peel
1 cup butter, at room temperature
1½ cups brown sugar, firmly packed
5 eggs, well beaten
¾ cup milk
2 cups fine dry bread crumbs
½ cup cognac or other good brandy
½ cup rum

Combine salt, nutmeg, and flour in a large mixing bowl. Add raisins, currants, citron, and orange peel and mix well so that all fruit is evenly coated with flour.

In a separate bowl, cream butter and sugar until light and fluffy. Add eggs and beat mixture until well blended.

In a large saucepan, heat the milk until steamy but not boiling. Add bread crumbs and mix well. Pour into cake batter and blend well. Add cognac and fruit-flour mixture. If batter seems too heavy add a little extra cognac or milk. Blend well.

Grease two 1-pound coffee tins very well with salad oil. Pour batter into tins, then cover tins with aluminum foil and tie tightly in place with kitchen string. Place tins on a rack in a large kettle and pour in water to come ¾ of the way up the tins. If the molds float, put a weight on them. Cover kettle and steam over medium heat (the water should just barely bubble) for 6 hours, adding more hot water as it evaporates.

Remove cake from tins by opening the bottom of each coffee can with a can opener and gently pushing the cake out. Pour the rum over the cakes and allow to cool slightly. If cakes are made ahead, replace them in fresh coffee tins and steam for 1 hour before serving.

If desired, cakes may be served flaming by sprinkling lightly with ultra-fine granulated sugar and 2 or 3 tablespoons of warmed brandy or rum. Ignite as soon as brandy or rum is poured over cake.

⊙

LOUISIANA AMBROSIA

14 large oranges
4 cups crushed pineapple, drained
4 cups canned or frozen coconut

With a sharp knife, cut each orange into 2 or 3 thick slices, discarding ends. Place orange slices on a chopping board and cut away skin and white membrane. Holding slices over a mixing bowl, divide them into sections, pulling away the white membrane and discarding this along with seeds. This is a juicy process, and by doing it over the bowl, the juice is retained. Combine orange pulp with pineapple and 3 cups of the coconut. Mix well.

Spoon mixture into serving dish, traditionally a silver bowl. Spread top evenly with remaining cup of coconut. Cover and refrigerate at least 4 hours before serving.

⊙

SAND TARTS

¼ pound butter, at room temperature
¼ cup confectioners sugar
1 teaspoon vanilla
1 cup flour
1 cup finely chopped pecans
Confectioners sugar

Preheat oven to 350° F.

Cream the butter with the sugar. Stir in the vanilla. Combine flour and nuts. Add this to the butter mixture and blend well.

Dust hands with flour. Pinch off small pieces of the dough and form into crescent shapes. Place crescents on ungreased baking sheet and bake in the preheated oven about 20 minutes or until firm.

Dust cookies with powdered sugar while still hot.
Makes about 36 cookies.

⊙

ELEGANT SOUTHERN BUFFET
FOR EIGHT OR TEN

AT THE BAR:
Champagne (in a silver ice bucket)

ON THE COFFEE TABLE:
Raw Crisp Vegetables (thin slices of turnip, cauliflower flowerettes, and zucchini straws on ice)

Remoulade Dip

Miniature Cheese Biscuits

ON THE BUFFET TABLE:
Platter of South County Baked Ham Slices Garnished with Fresh Pineapple Sticks and Sugared Grape Clusters

Charleston-style Scalloped Oysters

Broccoli Mousse

Chutney

Ripe and Green Olives

Miniature Rolls

DESSERT SERVED TO GUESTS AT THE TABLE:
Fresh Strawberries Brûlées

AFTER DINNER COFFEE IN THE LIVING ROOM:
Cointreau Filtre Coffee

○

SOUTH COUNTY BAKED HAM

The only problem confronting the cook in this recipe is in buying the ham—country-smoked, tenderized, ready-to-eat or full cooked, "dry cured" or "water added"—the language of ham is confusing. Confronted by supermarket variety, anyone may find a choice difficult to make.

For best flavor and slicing qualities, a dry-smoked (make sure the label does NOT read "water added") mildly cured ham is your best choice. It will be imprinted with the purple U.S. inspection stamp which means that it has been treated by approved methods to make sure no live trichinae remain in the meat. This stamp assures you that the ham does not need to be cooked for safety precautions but only to bring out the full, rich ham flavor.

Choose the butt end of the ham. It has the most sliceable meat. Ask the butcher to remove the rind and all but a thin layer of fat.

1 four- to five-pound half ham, dry-smoked, butt end
1 cup Coca-Cola
½ cup dry vermouth
½ cup fresh orange juice
½ cup honey
½ teaspoon ground cloves
½ teaspoon powdered mustard
½ cup powdered sugar

Preheat oven to 300° F.

Place ham in a shallow roasting pan. Pour Coca-Cola over ham surface. Place ham in preheated oven and bake 30 minutes to the pound, basting every 15 minutes. After 1 hour of cooking, pour over the ham the vermouth, orange juice, and honey. Sprinkle ham surface with cloves and mustard. Continue to baste ham every 15 minutes.

Ten minutes before ham is ready, remove it from the oven and spread confectioners sugar evenly over surface.

Increase oven temperature to 500° F. Return ham to oven and

bake until the sugar melts and forms a glaze, about 10 minutes.

Remove ham to serving platter and let come to room temperature before slicing.

NOTE: You can bake the ham well in advance of your party—one day, or even one week ahead—whenever it fits into your schedule. Store ham well wrapped in your refrigerator but bring again to room temperature before slicing to serve.

A whole ham may be baked in the same way—simply increase the liquid baste proportionally and decrease the baking time to 25 minutes to the pound.

In this recipe the fat is not scored. The traditional but oversweet (and, to my thinking, trite) garnish of pineapple rings and whole cloves has been eliminated because the ham will be sliced before serving.

⊙

CHARLESTON-STYLE SCALLOPED OYSTERS

3 tablespoons butter
1 tablespoon flour
1½ cups light cream
½ cup dry white wine or vermouth
½ teaspoon salt
¼ teaspoon pepper
1 large egg yolk, well beaten
1 quart small or medium oysters and their liquid
2 cups crumbled unsalted soda crackers
Butter slivers, about 1 tablespoon

Melt the butter in a heavy saucepan and stir in the flour. Cook, stirring, over low heat for a full minute. Slowly add the cream, stirring as it is added. Add the wine or vermouth. Season with salt and pepper and cook, stirring often, for about 5 minutes. Remove from heat and add the beaten egg yolk, again beating as it is added. Add the oysters and their liquid.

Butter an 8-inch by 12-inch shallow glass baking dish and cover bottom of dish with crumbled crackers. Pour in about ½ of the mixture and cover with crumbled crackers. Repeat with remaining oyster mixture and crumbs. Dot surface with slivers of butter.

If desired, refrigerate until ready to bake but for no more than 2 hours.

To bake, place baking dish in a pan with sufficient warm water to come halfway up sides of dish. Place in a preheated 325° F. oven and bake until firm, about 30 minutes.

NOTE: You may bake Scalloped Oysters up to one day ahead. Bake until just firm. Cover dish with foil and refrigerate as soon as taken from the oven. To reheat, place in cold oven in pan of warm water. Set oven temperature at 325° F. and bake only until thoroughly heated. Serve at once.

⊙

BROCCOLI MOUSSE

MOUSSE

2 *pounds fresh broccoli or 2 packages (10-ounce size) frozen broccoli*
3 *tablespoons butter*
3 *tablespoons flour*
1 *cup light cream*
5 *egg yolks*
¼ to ½ *teaspoon dried thyme (optional)*
½ *teaspoon salt*
¼ *teaspoon freshly ground pepper*
1 *teaspoon lemon juice*

TOPPING

¾ *cup fine dry bread crumbs*
¼ *cup grated Parmesan cheese*

Cook fresh broccoli according to directions on page 113. Drain, reserving ½ cup of cooking water. Chop fine. Cook frozen broccoli according to package directions.

Melt the butter in a large, heavy saucepan and stir in the flour. Cook over very low heat, stirring almost constantly with a wooden spoon for a full 2 minutes. Slowly add the cream, stirring as it is added. Stir in the ½ cup reserved cooking water and cook, still stirring, over low heat, to a medium-thick, smooth white sauce. Remove from heat. To keep a film from forming on the surface of the sauce, cover it with plastic wrap.

In a medium-to-large mixing bowl beat the egg yolks until they are 5 to 6 times their original volume (this takes about 5 minutes with a wire whisk or about 2 minutes with an electric beater). Add about 2 tablespoons of the still-warm white sauce, beating as it is added. Pour this into the cream sauce and blend with wire whisk or electric beater. Add the chopped broccoli, thyme, salt, pepper, and lemon juice. Blend.

Pour mixture into a well-buttered 2-quart soufflé mold.

Cover surface completely with topping of bread crumbs and grated cheese.

NOTE: Mousse may be prepared ahead to this point. Cover the top of the mold with aluminum foil and refrigerate until about 15 minutes before baking.

When ready to bake, set the soufflé mold in a large pan filled with sufficient warm water to extend approximately halfway up sides of mold. Place in a preheated 325° F. oven and bake for 1 hour or until firm.

HOW TO COOK FRESH BROCCOLI

Select tender young heads that are all green. A tinge of yellow bloom at the top means that the broccoli has been left too long in the ground and will be tough.

Remove and discard large outer leaves and the tough part of the stalk. Cut remaining stalks from heads. Cut stalks lengthwise into 2 or 4 pieces.

Place stalks and heads in cold water and soak for 10 minutes. Drain into a colander and rinse under cold running water. Drain.

Place ¾ cup of water in a large shallow enamelized cast-iron pan (one with a tight-fitting lid). Add broccoli stalks. Cover and steam until almost tender, 8 to 10 minutes. Add broccoli heads. Cover and steam until tender, about 3 additional minutes.

⊙

FRESH STRAWBERRIES BRÛLÉES

2 pints strawberries
2 tablespoons cognac
2 tablespoons confectioners sugar
1 pint commercial sour cream
2 cups light brown sugar

Wash and hull strawberries. Cut medium-size berries in half; quarter large berries. Place berries in bowl with cognac and confectioners sugar. Refrigerate, covered, for 1 hour or longer. Toss berries occasionally.

Preheat broiler to 500° F.

Spoon berries equally into the bottom of 8 individual custard cups and fill to about 1 inch of brim with sour cream. Sprinkle brown sugar evenly over each so that the sour cream is completely covered.

Place the filled custard cups in a long, shallow pan and surround them completely with crushed ice.

Place under broiler heat just long enough for the sugar to form a crust.

Keep the oven door open and watch constantly because the sugar scorches easily. Cool slightly, then cover each custard cup with foil and refrigerate 4 to 5 hours (or longer) before serving.

⊙

EASY BUDGET BUFFET FOR TWELVE

AT THE BAR:
Assortment of Imported Beer
(in an old-fashioned ice-filled bucket)

ON THE COFFEE TABLE:
Marinated Cauliflower Flowerettes and Green Olives on
Crushed Ice

Basket of Pretzel Sticks

ON THE BUFFET TABLE:
Casserole of New England Baked Beans

Spiced Green Bean and Celery Salad

Platter of Miniature Frankfurters on Parkerhouse Rolls
(with bowl of mustard dressing)

SIDEBOARD DESSERT:
Huguenot Apple-walnut Torte with Whipped Cream-cheese
Topping

Coffee

⊙

NEW ENGLAND BAKED BEANS

6 cups dried navy or pea beans
½ pound salt pork
2 small white onions, peeled and quartered
3 tablespoons dry mustard
6 tablespoons dark brown sugar
5 tablespoons molasses
3 tablespoons West Indies rum
3 cups (approximately) boiling water

Soak the beans in enough water to cover for 6 to 8 hours or overnight. Drain. Place beans in a 5- to 6-quart bean pot or two smaller bean pots.

Cut salt pork in two, scoring it in several places (if the pork is crusted with salt, rinse it under cold running water). Bury pork in the beans, along with the onion quarters.

Combine mustard, brown sugar, molasses, and rum; blend and pour over beans. Add enough boiling water to cover. Bake, covered, in a very slow—250° to 300° F.—oven for 8 to 10 hours or until beans are tender. Remove cover during the last hour of baking.

⊙

SPICED GREEN BEAN AND CELERY SALAD

1 cup cider vinegar
1 cup salad oil
6 whole cloves
1 tablespoon sugar
½ teaspoon salt
½ teaspoon black pepper
2 pounds fresh green beans
2 cups chopped celery
3 tablespoons minced onions
3 tablespoons minced parsley

Combine the vinegar, salad oil, cloves, sugar, salt, and pepper in a small bowl.

Wash beans and snap off string end. Bring a large kettle of water to a full, rolling boil. Add beans, a few at a time to avoid stopping the water from boiling. Cook 10 to 15 minutes or until just tender. Drain beans at once and immediately cover them with cold water to stop the cooking process.

Combine still-warm beans with celery and minced onion. Remove cloves from dessing and pour over salad. Cover and refrigerate for at least 6 hours or overnight. Just before serving, sprinkle salad with minced parsley.

⊙

HUGUENOT APPLE-WALNUT TORTE WITH WHIPPED CREAM-CHEESE TOPPING

TORTE
6 eggs
4 cups sugar
12 tablespoons flour
6 teaspoons baking powder
¾ teaspoon salt
3 cups chopped tart cooking apples
3 cups chopped walnuts
3 teaspoons cognac

Preheat oven to 325° F.

Grease two 8 inch by 12 inch by 2 inch baking pans with salad oil.

Beat the eggs until very frothy. Add sugar, flour, baking powder, and salt and beat until well blended.

Add walnuts, apples, and cognac and blend well. Pour mixture into prepared pans and bake in preheated oven about 40 minutes or until brown and crusty. Cut torte into serving sections and serve directly from baking dish if desired.

TOPPING
2 six-ounce packages cream cheese
½ cup milk
Allow cream cheese to come to room temperature. Combine with milk and beat to a smooth consistency. Refrigerate until ready to serve.

⊙

CARIBBEAN BUFFET FOR TWELVE

AT THE BAR:
Barbados Punch

ON THE COFFEE TABLE:
Toasted Almonds

Cheese Straws

ON THE BUFFET TABLE:
Trinidad Creamed Turkey with Pineapple and Almonds

Toast Points

Island Barbequed Spareribs

Raw Vegetable Platter with Avocado Dip

Guava Jelly

Planters Coconut Cake

Coffee spiked with Rum

All recipes for this menu can be easily doubled to serve 24 guests.

⊙

BARBADOS PUNCH

2 bottles (fifths) light rum
1 quart unsweetened canned pineapple juice
2 bottles (fifths) sauterne
1 ounce bitters
3 quarts dry champagne
1 seedless orange, peeled and sliced
½ pint fresh strawberries, hulled, washed and sliced
6 slices fresh or canned pineapple

Mix together the rum, pineapple juice, sauterne, and bitters. Cover and refrigerate 4 hours or longer. Pour liquid over block of ice in punch bowl. Pour in champagne and add fruit just before serving.

About 36 punch-cups of punch.

○

TRINIDAD CREAMED TURKEY WITH PINEAPPLE AND ALMONDS

¼ *pound butter*
½ *cup flour*
2 *cups heated chicken or turkey stock or broth (homemade is best but canned will do)*
½ *cup dry sherry*
2 *cups light cream*
1 *teaspoon salt (less if stock or broth is salty)*
¼ *teaspoon pepper*
1 *teaspoon grated onion*
3 *cups cooked diced turkey*
1 *cup shredded (fresh or canned) pineapple, well drained*
½ *cup toasted slivered almonds*
Toast points or hot noodles

Melt the butter in a large enamelized cast-iron pot. Add the flour and stir over very low heat until blended and smooth.

Remove pot from heat and slowly add the heated stock or broth, stirring with a wire whisk as it is added. Add sherry and cream. Blend well and return pan to heat. Stir (still over low heat) until mixture is uniformly thickened. Season with salt, pepper, and onion.

NOTE: Recipe can be made ahead to this point. Cover sauce directly with plastic wrap to keep film from forming. Refrigerate until ready to reheat, or place pot in a large pan of hot water over very low heat, stirring frequently to keep film from forming; keep hot until ready to continue with recipe.

Add turkey, pineapple, and almonds. Bring to steaming hot and transfer to serving dish.

Serve over toast points or, if preferred, over flat noodles cooked according to package directions.

⊙

ISLAND BARBEQUED SPARERIBS

6 pounds spareribs
½ cup soy sauce
½ cup chicken stock or broth
3 tablespoons hoisin sauce (available in Chinese grocery stores
or gourmet food shops)
⅓ cup brown sugar
3 cloves garlic, peeled and crushed
1 teaspoon ground ginger
1 teaspoon dry mustard
   OR
2 teaspoons Chinese five-spice powder

Preheat oven to 350° F.

Place spareribs on rack in a flat roasting pan. Roast in pre-heated 350° F. oven for 1 hour. Remove from heat.

Combine remaining ingredients in a saucepan. Place over low heat and stir until sugar dissolves. *Do not allow to boil.*

Cut meat into individual ribs. Remove and discard fat in pan and put back ribs without the rack. Pour soy sauce mixture over ribs.

Increase oven temperature to 375° F. and bake ribs for 45 minutes to 1 hour, turning and basting them frequently.

Serve ribs hot or at room temperature.

TO PREPARE AHEAD: Roast ribs for 1 hour, then bake as directed with sauce for 15 minutes. Remove from heat. Cover baking pan and let stand at room temperature for up to 4 hours, then bake before serving for a final 30 minutes.

⊙

AVOCADO DIP

1 large tomato
3 ripe avocadoes
½ cup mayonnaise (p. 71)
3 tablespoons lime juice
Salt
½ teaspoon ground coriander seed (optional)
2 teaspoons (or to taste) bottled red or green salsa jalapeno
    (hot chili sauce)

Plunge tomato in boiling water for ½ minute, then hold under cold water and slip off skin. Cut tomato in half and gently squeeze out seeds and juice. (You may save this for another use.) Cut tomato halves into thin strips.

Peel avocados and cut in half. Remove seeds (reserving them). Place avocados in mixing bowl and mash until smooth. Add tomato strips and remaining ingredients.

Add reserved avocado seeds to mixture. (The seeds prevent the avocado from turning dark.) Cover the bowl and refrigerate until chilled. Remove seeds and spoon mixture into serving bowl.

Makes about 2 cups of dip.

⊙

PLANTERS COCONUT CAKE

CAKE
1 package Angel Food cake mix
1½ cups flaked toasted coconut
2 tablespoons light rum
½ cup guava jelly

Prepare Angel Food cake mix according to package directions. Fold ½ cup of the coconut and the rum into finished batter. Bake as directed. Cool. Remove cake from pan. Let stand for 1 hour, then cut horizontally into 2 layers. Spread bottom layer with guava jelly, then cover jelly with top layer of cake. Spread Seven-minute Frosting (recipe below) over top and sides of cake. Sprinkle with remaining coconut.

SEVEN-MINUTE FROSTING

One of the easiest and nicest icings. It never fails and has a delicious light crust while remaining creamy soft underneath. It adapts well to just about any traditional flavoring or to such innovations as grated orange or lemon peel, crushed peppermints, and slivered almonds.

> 2 egg whites
> 1¾ cups sugar
> 5 tablespoons cold water
> ¼ teaspoon cream of tartar
> 1 teaspoon flavoring

Combine ingredients (except flavoring) in top half of a double boiler over rapidly boiling water. Beat constantly with a wire whisk for 6 to 7 minutes. Remove from heat. Add flavoring and beat until thick enough to spread. Add nuts, peel, or any extra ingredient just before spreading on cake.

Makes about 2 cups of icing.

○

BUDGET FUND-RAISING BUFFET
FOR TWENTY-FOUR

AT THE BAR:
Draft Beer
(served in old-time beer-parlor mugs)

AT THE SALAD BUFFET TABLE:
Danish Cucumber Salad

Planky
(Russian Bean Salad)

Braunschwieger Schloss Salad
(Swiss Cheese and Frankfurter Salad)

Buttered Cocktail Rye Bread Rounds

Assorted Crackers

Carrot and Celery Sticks on Crushed Ice

ON THE HOT-FOOD BUFFET TABLE:
Irish Lamb Stew

Hot Crusty Rolls

ON THE DESSERT TABLE:
Apple Crisp with Lemon Sauce

Coffee

This is a very satisfactory hearty menu for club or church-group efforts. Form a food committee, putting one person in charge, and farm out the recipes. (They are all easy to prepare, can be made ahead, and can easily be doubled or even tripled to serve 50 or 70 persons.) Place another person in charge of setting the table and seeing that the food arrives ahead of the guests.

All salads are actually at their best in flavor if served at room temperature.

As the Irish Lamb Stew is prepared in four pans of manageable size, they can be brought to the buffet one at a time, hot from the oven as needed.

⊙

DANISH CUCUMBER SALAD

SALAD INGREDIENTS
12 medium-size cucumbers
1 tablespoon salt
1 teaspoon tumeric
2 cups water
2 cups white wine vinegar

DRESSING
1 cup sour cream
1 cup mayonnaise (page 71)
1 teaspoon grated onion with juice
1 tablespoon minced parsley

GARNISH
2 cups raisins that have been plumped in hot water, drained,
  and cooled
24 crisp lettuce leaves

Peel cucumbers. Slice on bias into ovals about ⅛-inch thick.

Mix salt and tumeric in an extralarge nonmetal bowl. Add water, vinegar, and cucumbers. Mix well. Refrigerate 2 to 3 hours. Stir occasionally.

Combine sour cream, mayonnaise, onion, and parsley.

Drain cucumbers and spoon into lettuce leaves arranged on serving platter. Top each salad with dressing and sprinkle generously with raisins.

⊙

PLANKY
(RUSSIAN BEAN SALAD)

2½ cups large dry white navy beans
1 teaspoon salt
¾ cup olive oil
2 cloves garlic, peeled and minced
2 carrots, scraped and chopped
4 stalks celery, thinly sliced
2 teaspoons chopped fresh dill or 1 teaspoon dried dill
½ cup chopped parsley
½ cup lemon juice
Salt
Freshly ground black pepper
Lemon wedges

Wash beans and soak them overnight in water to cover. Transfer beans and soaking water to a large pot and add sufficient water to cover. Bring beans slowly to a boil and let simmer until tender, about 2 hours. Add salt for the last 30 minutes of cooking. Drain beans and place them in a salad bowl.

Heat oil in a small skillet. Add garlic, carrots, and celery. Cook over low heat, stirring frequently, for 15 minutes. Pour over cooked beans. Add remaining ingredients. Blend gently but thoroughly.

Garnish with lemon wedges.

⊙

BRAUNSCHWIEGER SCHLOSS SALAD
(SWISS CHEESE AND FRANKFURTER SALAD)

SALAD INGREDIENTS
3 pounds Swiss cheese
3 pounds frankfurters
3 large dill pickles
2 large mild purple onions

DRESSING
1 cup salad oil
½ cup white wine vinegar
2 tablespoons prepared mustard
2 teaspoons salt
1 teaspoon pepper
1 tablespoon sugar

GARNISH
Lettuce leaves
Tomato wedges

Slice cheese and cut slices into narrow strips. Slice frankfurters and pickles into thin rounds. Peel and slice onions, breaking slices into rings. Place cheese, frankfurters, pickles, and onion rings in mixing bowl.

Combine oil, vinegar, mustard, salt, pepper, and sugar. Beat with wire whisk until frothy. Pour over salad ingredients in mixing bowl. Toss well. Refrigerate until chilled.

Line salad bowl with lettuce leaves. Fill with chilled salad. Garnish with tomato wedges.

⊙

IRISH LAMB STEW

Irish stew can be bland and insipid, or it can be sublime. It depends on the liquid used in its cooking. This liquid is absorbed by both the potatoes and meat, so it should never be water but a rich flavorful stock. I use a simple fat-free meat stock that can be made a day, a week, or even a month ahead. The making of the stew itself is just a matter of assembling the ingredients. It is a great dish for serving a crowd because it can be made in any quantity as long as you have sufficient baking dishes and oven space.

6 pounds of lean lamb
6 large mild purple onions
12 pounds best-quality baking potatoes
Salt
Pepper
Minced parsley
10 cups meat stock, fresh or canned

Cut the meat into 1½-inch cubes.

Peel and cut onions and potatoes into about ¼-inch slices.

Cover the bottom of four 12-inch by 8-inch by 6-inch baking pans with potato slices. Add a few onion slices. Sprinkle with salt, pepper, and parsley; cover with lamb cubes. Repeat this twice, ending with potatoes. Over this (if the stew is to be served as soon as it is ready), pour 2½ cups of stock.

Cover and seal each filled pan with foil. Place in a preheated 350° F. oven and bake about 3 hours or until all liquid has been absorbed but potatoes are still moist.

If stew is to be baked ahead and then reheated, reduce liquid to 2 cups. Cool slightly; then refrigerate, covered. Remove from refrigerator about 1 hour and let stand at room temperature before reheating. Pour remaining stock (½ cup for each pan) over potatoes and meat, then cover and seal with fresh foil. Place in cold oven. Set temperature at 350° F. and bake until thoroughly heated (30 to 45 minutes).

Stew can be made 1 to 2 days ahead. Freezing is *not* recommended.

⊙

APPLE CRISP WITH LEMON SAUCE

Butter, at room temperature
12 medium-size McIntosh or other crisp apples
¾ cup lemon juice
2¼ cups quick-cooking oatmeal
1½ cups flour
1½ cups brown sugar
1½ cups butter
¾ cup corn syrup

Generously butter three 8-inch by 12-inch by 2-inch glass baking pans.

Peel, core, and slice apples. Arrange in overlapping layers in baking dishes. Sprinkle with lemon juice.

Combine oatmeal, flour, and sugar in mixing bowl. Cut in 1½ cups of butter. Add syrup and blend well.

Sprinkle ⅓ of mixture evenly over each pan of apples.

NOTE: Recipe can be prepared ahead to this point.

Refrigerate until 30 minutes before time to bake. Bake in a preheated 350° F. oven for 25 to 30 minutes or until crisp.

Serve warm with Lemon Sauce (recipe below).

LEMON SAUCE

3 cups sugar
3 cups boiling water
⅛ teaspoon salt
3 tablespoons cornstarch
½ cup (1 stick) butter, at room temperature
½ cup lemon juice
1 tablespoon grated lemon rind

Combine sugar, cornstarch, and salt in top of double boiler. Use a wooden spoon to blend these ingredients together. Slowly add the boiling water, stirring vigorously as it is added. Cook, stirring almost constantly, over moderate heat until mixture is smooth and thickened. Remove from heat and add room-temperature butter. Stir until butter has melted. Add lemon juice and rind.

Keep warm over simmering water until ready to serve. Or cover sauce directly with plastic wrap to prevent film from forming, cover pan, and refrigerate until ready to serve. Reheat over simmering water.

Makes about 4 cups of sauce.

⊙

SUMMER TERRACE BUFFET FOR TWELVE, ON A BUDGET

Cold Glazed Meatloaf Slices with Mustard Pickles
Potato Salad with Dill and Ripe Olives
Hot Casserole of Texas Hill Country Baked Beans
Corn Sticks
Iced Bowl of Raw Vegetables (carrot sticks, cucumber fingers,
cherry tomatoes, cauliflower flowerets, ripe Greek olives)
Coarse Salt for Dipping
Cold Beer
Pineapple Skillet Cake
Coffee

⊙

GLAZED MEATLOAF

3 pounds ground round steak
½ pound pork sausage meat
2 tablespoons butter
½ cup very finely chopped onions
½ cup very finely chopped celery
½ cup very finely chopped green peppers
3 tablespoons fine, dry bread crumbs
2 eggs, well beaten
1 cup tomato ketchup
2 teaspoons salt
½ teaspoon pepper
½ cup chili sauce
½ cup currant jelly

Preheat oven to 350° F.

Combine round steak and sausage meat in a mixing bowl.

Melt butter in a skillet. Add onions, celery, and green peppers. Cook, stirring, until vegetables are limp.

With a rubber spatula, scrape the entire contents of the skillet over the meats. Add the bread crumbs, eggs, ketchup, salt, and pepper. Blend the mixture thoroughly.

Shape into two loaves. Place on baking sheet in center of oven and bake in preheated oven for 1½ hours.

Last 30 minutes of baking: Heat chili sauce with currant jelly. Pour ½ of mixture over loaves. Bake for 15 minutes, then pour remaining mixture over loaves and bake for final 15 minutes.

○

POTATO SALAD WITH DILL AND RIPE OLIVES

4 pounds new potatoes
2 cups homemade mayonnaise (page 71)
2 tablespoons fresh lemon juice
2 tablespoons minced shallots
2 cups finely diced celery
3 hard-cooked eggs, coarsely chopped
½ cup finely minced sweet pickles
2 teaspoons salt
1 teaspoon black pepper
1 tablespoon dry mustard
1 tablespoon minced fresh dill
24 black olives

Scrub the potatoes and cook in boiling water until tender. Do not allow potatoes to overcook or the salad will be mushy. Peel and cut into cubes. While still warm, combine potatoes with mayonnaise and lemon juice and toss well. Add remaining ingredients and toss again to blend. Refrigerate for at least 4 hours before serving. Garnish with fresh dill and ripe olives.

○

TEXAS HILL COUNTRY BAKED BEANS

2 pounds (4 cups) great northern or pea beans
3 to 4 quarts water
1 can (1 pound) tomatoes
¾ cup tomato ketchup
⅓ cup dark brown sugar
2 teaspoons chili powder
2 teaspoons dry mustard
2 teaspoons salt
¼ cup red wine vinegar
3 medium onions, peeled and chopped
½ pound salt pork, cut into cubes

Place beans in a heavy 4-quart oven casserole that can also be used over direct heat. Cover with about 3 inches of cold water. Place over high heat and bring to a full boil. Let boil for 2 minutes, skimming surface of water until clear.

Remove casserole from heat and let stand at room temperature for 1 hour. Return to moderate heat, cover, and let simmer gently for 45 minutes.

Drain beans through a colander over a large bowl. Return the beans to the casserole. Reserve cooking water.

Pour 2 cups of the cooking water into a second large bowl. Add the tomatoes, ketchup, sugar, chili powder, mustard, salt, and vinegar. Blend with a whisk, then pour over beans in casserole. Add the chopped onion and the salt pork cubes; gently mix them into the beans.

Place casserole again over direct heat and bring liquid to a full boil.

Cover and place casserole in a preheated (375° F.) oven. Bake for 2 hours, then add 1 cup of the reserved cooking water. Bake, covered, for an additional 1 hour, then uncover and continue to bake until beans are tender but not falling apart, about 30 minutes.

If necessary, add additional cooking water to keep beans moist while baking.

○

CORN STICKS

1½ cups cornmeal
2 cups flour
½ teaspoon salt
4 teaspoons baking powder
2 eggs, lightly beaten
2 cups milk
¼ cup bacon drippings
½ cup crumbled crisp cooked bacon

Preheat oven to 450° F.

Grease three 6-stick iron cornstick pans very well with salad oil or bacon drippings.

Place in oven to get very hot.

Combine cornmeal and flour with remaining ingredients. Stir until well blended. Pour into heated pans and bake in preheated oven for 10 to 15 minutes or until firm and lightly browned. Turn out at once on rack to cool. May be reheated in a low oven if desired.

⊙

PINEAPPLE SKILLET CAKE

½ cup butter
½ cup brown sugar
5 slices canned pineapple, drained
½ cup chopped pecans
5 maraschino cherries
1 package (18½ ounces) yellow cake mix
1 package (3¾ ounces) vanilla pudding mix
½ cup rum
½ cup vegetable oil
4 eggs, lightly beaten

Preheat oven to 350° F.

Melt the butter and combine with brown sugar. Spread mixture evenly over the bottom of a heavy 10-inch skillet. Arrange the pineapple slices over the sugar. Center each slice with a cherry.

Combine cake mix with pudding mix, rum, oil, and eggs. Beat well with electric mixer for 2 minutes (or for 6 minutes by hand). Pour over pineapple-sugar combination and bake for 50 to 60 minutes or until cake tests done.

Allow to cool for 5 minutes before inverting onto a serving plate.

Smorgasbord

⊙

Like all foreign food customs that have come to this country, the smorgasbord has been adapted to American ways. The word *smorgasbord* is now used interchangably with buffet and can mean any self-service meal. But when the Old World menu is faithfully followed, the smorgasbord is another thing entirely—an out-of-this-country experience, easy to prepare yet a real adventure in dining.

TRADITION

The pattern for an authentic smorgasbord has been perfected over five hundred years of historic eating, and tradition requires that it be followed precisely. First, the table must contain the required sixty items, to be divided among four courses. Herring and other cold smoked or pickled fish along with other cold fish dishes start the meal. Next are salads and cold meats with their accompanying pickles and relishes. The third course consists of a variety of hot dishes. Finally, there is an assortment of cheeses. Dishes are arranged on the table in related groups. If dessert and coffee are added to the menu, they are placed on a separate table. They are not a traditional part of the meal.

TABLE DECOR

Careful thought should be given to table arrangements. Flowers and candles are used to add color and drama, but the food itself is the "main attraction." Each dish should be decorative. Ham slices, roast beef slices, or other cold cuts can be arranged on platters and decorated with sprigs of parsley. The sliced salmon should be rolled up and topped with a twisted lemon slice. Salads should be in lettuce-lined bowls; the caviar and raw vegetables set in bowls of crushed ice. Added effect can be achieved by presenting unusual and attractively packaged imported foods in their original containers. The cans should be opened and the lids neatly rolled back to show the contents—each can on a separate small plate and the plate garnished with a few sprigs of fresh dill, radish roses, or watercress. The hot foods should be in good-looking casseroles on warming trays or in silver (or silver-plated) chafing dishes over candle warmers.

Plates, silver, and napkins are placed at one end of the table. Provide four small (salad-size) plates, four forks, knives as needed, and several changes of napkins for each guest. Tradition dictates that each course be eaten on a separate clean plate and with clean silver. Piling up a plate with unrelated foods, then going back for more with the same plate, is unthinkable at this most casual yet most ritualistic of meals.

PARTY STRATEGY

The first step in preparing a smorgasbord is a trip to the best gourmet food shop in your town for as many kinds of imported herring as you can find. Next, select a variety of other imported smoked and pickled fish: tiny Icelandic shrimp, rolled anchovies, sardines in mustard or tomato sauce, smoked oysters, red salmon, caviar, etc. Then, as the sky is the limit at a smorgasbord and the idea is to have not only variety but foods that are not normally served at home, do as your Scandinavian counterpart would do: add as many interesting and exciting delicacies as you can afford. Your total purchases should make up at least 75 or 80 percent of the required sixty items to be served.

In addition to herring and other fish, and pickles and relishes, every smorgasbord must have its assortment of breads. You will want to add to your shopping cart: light and dark rye, pumpernickel and Norwegian flat bread, as well as rye crisp and unsalted crackers for cheese—and the cheese itself. For this item, buy whole cheese wedges or blocks of cheese; smorgasbord cheese is never served sliced but left whole or in large pieces for the guest to cut to his individual choice.

With such an assortment of food already prepared and ready to serve, there is little actual cooking to be done for this party meal. How much you will cook depends on you. The following menu keeps to tradition, with four salads and three hot dishes. Dessert has been included as most people, especially men, like to end the meal with a sweet. And there's coffee, of course, for the last drink of the night.

⊙

AN AUTHENTIC SMORGASBORD
FOR TWENTY-FOUR

AT THE BAR:
Akvavit on Ice

Assortment of Scandinavian Beer

ON THE STILL BOARD:
Matjes Herring

Glassmasters Herring

Herring in Sour Cream

Smoked Nova Scotia Salmon

Red Salmon Caviar

Tiny Icelandic Shrimp

Smoked Oysters

Smoked Whitefish

Thin Slices of Dark and Light Bread

Butter Balls

Cocktail Sauces

ON THE SMORGASBORD TABLE:
Scandinavian Cucumbers

Potato Salad

Viking Salad

Swedish Coleslaw

Relishes

Celery Sticks

Radish Roses

Carrot Curls

Pickled Mushrooms

Pickled Cauliflower

Assorted Olives

Swiss Cheese

Norwegian Rindless Cheese

Tilsiter Cheese

Nokkel Ost (Pickled Cheese with Caraway)

Cold Sliced Baked Turkey, Chicken, and Roast Beef

Danish Ham

Norwegian Salami

Sylta (Head Cheese)

Liver Paste

Sour Cream

Prepared Horseradish

Lingonberries

Pickled Peaches

Pickled Pears

Swedish Meatballs

Janson's Temptation

Boiled Potatoes with Fresh Dill

Light and Dark Rye Bread, Pumpernickel

Norwegian Flat Bread

Rye Crisp

Unsalted Crackers

Butter Balls

ON THE DESSERT TABLE:

Mixed Swedish Berries Marinated in Kirsch

Scandinavian Butter Cookies

Coffee

⊙

SMORGASBORD AMERICAN STYLE
FOR TWENTY-FOUR

AT THE BAR:

Akvavit on Ice

Assortment of Imported Beer

AT THE STILL BOARD:

Marinated Herring

Norwegian Anchovies

Smoked Nova Scotia Salmon

Light and Dark Rye Bread

ON THE SMORGASBORD TABLE:

Viking Salad

Potato Salad

Assorted Olives

Assorted Pickles

Celery Sticks

Carrot Curls

Swiss Cheese

Tilsiter Cheese

Danish Ham

Sour Cream with Chopped Dill

Prepared Horseradish

Swedish Meatballs

Janson's Temptation

Light and Dark Rye Bread

Rye Crisp

Unsalted Crackers

ON THE DESSERT TABLE:

Mixed Swedish Berries marinated in Kirsch

Scandinavian Butter Cookies

Coffee

○

VIKING SALAD

DRESSING
½ cup white wine vinegar
1½ cups salad oil
1 egg yolk
1 tablespoon heavy cream
1 teaspoon minced chives
Salt
Freshly ground black pepper to taste

SALAD
2 pounds boiled shrimp, peeled and deveined
2 pounds lump crabmeat
4 flat cans (4 ounces) smoked oysters
1 head Boston lettuce, torn into bite-size chunks
3 cups cooked green peas, fresh or frozen

GARNISH
Tomato wedges
Fresh dill sprigs

Combine vinegar and oil and blend with a wire whisk. Beat egg yolk with cream; add to vinegar and oil, beating as this is added. Add chives and season to taste with salt and pepper.

Combine salad ingredients in serving bowl. Add dressing and toss lightly but thoroughly. Cover and refrigerate at least 1 hour before serving to allow flavors to blend.

Garnish bowl with tomato wedges and fresh dill sprigs.

⊙

SWEDISH COLESLAW

2 large heads green cabbage, finely shredded
20 crisp radishes, trimmed and very thinly sliced
3 carrots, scraped and grated
1 small green pepper with all white removed, cut into thinnest
   possible slivers
1 teaspoon sugar
1 teaspoon salt
1½ cups mayonnaise (page 71)
1 cup sour cream
1 tablespoon caraway seeds
1 teaspoon prepared mustard

Combine shredded cabbage, radish slices, grated carrots, and green pepper slivers in salad bowl. Sprinkle with sugar and salt. Toss well.

Combine mayonnaise, sour cream, caraway seeds, and mustard. Blend, then add to slaw mixture. Toss again. Cover and refrigerate 2 hours or longer before serving.

⊙

JANSON'S TEMPTATION
(SCALLOPED POTATOES SWEDISH STYLE)

10 large Idaho potatoes
2 small cans (2-ounce size) anchovy fillets
1 cup minced onions
½ teaspoon pepper
¼ cup (½ stick) butter
4 cups light cream

Preheat oven to 350° F.

Scrub potatoes clean with a stiff vegetable brush. Scrape away any discolored spots but do not peel. Cut into the thinnest possible slices.

Drain and chop anchovy fillets. Butter two long shallow baking dishes and place a layer of potatoes in the bottom of each. Top with anchovy fillets and sprinkle with minced onions and pepper.

Dot with slivers of the butter and cover with a second layer of potatoes. Pour 2 cups of the cream over each mixture and dot with the remaining butter.

Bake in preheated oven for about 30 minutes or until potatoes are tender. Place briefly under broiler heat to brown surface.

⊙

SWEDISH MEATBALLS

3 slices (1-inch thick) firm white bread cut from a whole loaf
Milk, as needed
2 tablespoons butter
½ cup finely minced onions
1 pound ground veal
1 pound ground lean pork
1 pound ground round steak
4 eggs, well beaten
2 teaspoons salt
2 teaspoons Worcestershire sauce
2 teaspoons lemon juice
1 teaspoon sugar
¼ teaspoon ground cloves
8 cups beef stock, fresh or canned (more if needed)
4 tablespoons butter
4 tablespoons flour
1 cup sour cream
1 bottle (2 ounces) capers, drained

Place bread in a bowl. Add enough milk to just cover. Let soak 1 hour.

Sauté onions in butter until soft.

Combine meats in a large mixing bowl.

Press milk from bread and add bread to meats. Add beaten eggs, sautéed onions, and all seasonings. Blend mixture lightly with two forks.

Place stock in a large heavy pot over medium heat. Bring to boil.

While stock heats, moisten hands with cold water and shape meat mixture into small, bite-size balls. Keep hands moist while you work.

Drop ⅓ of the meatballs into the hot stock. Cover and let

simmer for about 15 minutes. Remove with slotted spoon. Repeat until all have been cooked.

NOTE: Recipe can be prepared ahead to this point. Spoon about one cup of the stock over the meatballs. Cover and refrigerate until ready to continue. Cover and refrigerate stock.

Reheat 6 cups of the stock. In another pot, melt the butter and stir in the flour. Cook, stirring over low heat, for about 5 minutes. Slowly stir in the hot stock. Cook over low heat, stirring often, until mixture is thick and smooth. Add the meatballs. When meatballs are heated, gently stir in the sour cream and the capers.

Transfer to chafing dish over hot water or large casserole on warming tray. Keep hot until ready to serve.

⊙

ITALIAN BUFFET FOR EIGHT

AT THE BAR:
Dry Cinzano
Lemon Peel Slivers
Soda

ON A SIDE TABLE:
Clams on the Half Shell on Crushed Ice
Cocktail Sauces
Lemon Wedges
Tabasco Sauce

ON THE MAIN TABLE:
Antipasto Platter
Lasagne Imbottite
Eggplant and Tomato Casserole
Parmesan Noodle Casserole

ON THE DESSERT TABLE:
Biscuit Tortoni
Whole Tangerines
Fresh Roasted Peanuts
Espresso

Recipes for this menu are for 8 servings but may easily be doubled to serve 16.

⊙

ANTIPASTO

Making an antipasto platter is a work of art. The trick is to arrange the various items attractively, with an eye for color, pattern, and texture. Here are the most popular antipasto foods. Pick the combination that appeals to you, keeping in mind that this is a salad so greenery and vegetables should make up one-half of your platter while eggs, meat, and fish comprise the remaining half. Pickled peppers and olives count as vegetables.

> *Lettuce wedges*
> *Quartered tomatoes*
> *Artichoke hearts*
> *Celery hearts*
> *Radishes*
> *Pimento-stuffed green olives*
> *Ripe olives (Italian variety if possible)*
> *Small green pickled peppers*
> *Sautéed small mushrooms (marinated in oil and vinegar and*
>   *served cold)*
> *Pimentos*
> *Thin slices of prosciutto*
> *Thin slices of pepperoni sausage (check your best Italian gro-*
>   *cery for additional sausage available; they are all good)*
> *Thin slices of Italian salami*
> *Tuna fish, broken into chunks*
> *Anchovy fillets*
> *Sardines*
> *Hard-cooked egg quarters*

Arrange your platter ahead of time. Sprinkle lightly with olive oil and vinegar. Cover tightly with plastic wrap and refrigerate until ready to serve.

⊙

LASAGNE IMBOTTITE
(STUFFED LASAGNE)

This recipe is very easy to prepare but it does take time. It can be prepared ahead, however, and if desired, the sauce may be made one day, the lasagne the next.

You may substitute ground meat for the minced meat but the minced meat is superior in flavor and does give the sauce a better texture.

> 1½ pounds lean chuck or round steak in one piece
> 1 clove garlic, peeled and minced
> 1 large purple (Italian) onion, peeled and minced
> ½ cup olive oil
> 1 can (1 lb. 12 oz.) Italian-style tomatoes with basil
> 4 cups beef stock
> 3 tablespoons Italian imported tomato purée
> ½ cup chopped parsley
> 1 teaspoon oregano
> ½ teaspoon pepper
> 1 teaspoon salt
> Water if needed
> 2 pounds lasagne
> Oil
> 2 pints Ricotta cheese, at room temperature
> 2 tablespoons milk, at room temperature
> 1½ pounds Mozzarella cheese, thinly sliced
> 1 pound freshly grated Parmesan cheese

Place meat in freezer until very firm. With a sharp knife, mince it finely (or have your butcher do this for you).

In a large heavy skillet sauté the garlic and onion in the oil until limp. Add the meat and cook, stirring until no longer pink. Add tomatoes, stock, tomato puree, parsley, oregano, salt, and pepper. Blend them well and let simmer over low heat for 1½ hours. Stir often and add a little water if sauce becomes overly thick.

Cook lasagne strips according to package directions, but adding 1 teaspoon of the oil to cooking water. When the lasagne is just tender, place the pot in the sink and let a thin trickle of cold water run into the pot until the lasagne has cooled. Remove lasagne strips and place side by side in single layer on a well-buttered baking sheet.

Combine the Ricotta cheese with the milk and beat until smooth.

Reheat sauce.

If the lasagne is to be baked at once, preheat oven to 350° F.

Cover the bottom of four 8-inch by 12-inch pans with a thin layer of sauce. Cover sauce with a layer of lasagne strips. Spread strips with Ricotta cheese. Top with a layer of Mozzarella cheese. Sprinkle with Parmesan cheese and top with the sauce. Repeat until all ingredients have been used, ending with a thick layer of sauce and a heavy sprinkling of Parmesan cheese.

NOTE: Recipe can be made ahead to this point. Let stand 1 to 2 hours at room temperature, or cover and refrigerate until 2 hours before baking.

Bake, uncovered, in preheated 350° F. oven until bubbly hot. Place under direct heat for a few seconds to brown surface. Will stay hot before cutting for 1 hour.

⊙

PARMESAN NOODLE CASSEROLE

1 package (1 pound) green noodles
½ cup butter, at room temperature
½ cup freshly grated Parmesan cheese
2 tablespoons chopped chives
2 tablespoons chopped parsley
2 eggs, lightly beaten
2 cups milk

Preheat oven to 300° F.

Prepare noodles according to package directions. Drain well into a large mixing bowl. Add butter and toss lightly with a fork until butter is evenly distributed.

Place a layer of noodles in a deep baking dish. Sprinkle with cheese, chives, and parsley, and repeat until all ingredients are used, ending with a layer of noodles. Combine eggs with milk and pour over casserole.

NOTE: Recipe can be prepared ahead to this point and refrigerated until 30 minutes before baking.

Bake for 40 to 45 minutes or until firm.

○

EGGPLANT AND TOMATO CASSEROLE

2 large eggplants
Salt
4 large tomatoes
1 small purple (Italian) onion
1 clove garlic, peeled
½ cup olive oil
½ cup butter
¾ cup chopped Mozzarella cheese
½ cup freshly grated Parmesan cheese
½ cup fine dry bread crumbs

Peel eggplant and cut into small (½-inch) cubes. Sprinkle with salt and let stand in a colander, topped with a heavy plate, for 30 minutes. Turn out onto paper toweling and pat dry.

Chop tomatoes. Peel and chop onion.

Preheat oven to 375° F.

Heat oil and butter in a large heavy skillet. Add garlic and cook 1 minute, then remove and discard garlic. Fry eggplant cubes, a few at a time, until golden on all sides. Arrange one layer of eggplant in a deep baking dish. Top with tomatoes and sprinkle with onion then Mozzarella and Parmesan cheeses. Repeat until all ingredients are used, ending with tomatoes and cheese.

NOTE: Recipe can be made ahead to this point. Cover baking dish with foil or plastic wrap. Can be kept at room temperature for 1 hour or stored in the refrigerator for 2 to 3 hours. But bring to room temperature before baking.

Bake, uncovered, in preheated 375° F. oven for 20 minutes or until hot and bubbly.

⊙

BISCUIT TORTONI

2 cups heavy cream
¾ cups powdered sugar
2 egg whites
1 cup crumbled macaroon crumbs
½ cup marsala or other sweet wine

Whip cream until stiff. Fold in powdered sugar.

Whip egg whites until stiff. Fold egg whites into cream, alternating with ¾ of the macaroon crumbs and the marsala. Pack the mixture into small paper muffin cups. Sprinkle remaining crumbs over surface. Set cups on a large baking sheet and place in freezer until firm. Wrap individually in plastic wrap. Store in freezer.

NOTE: Cups should be placed on buffet table about 1 hour before serving.

Formal
Dinner Parties

⊙

The first formal dinner party I ever attended was one of the most pleasurable events of my life. I was invited as a member of the press—at the time I was a newspaper columnist—to a dinner party given by the Countess de Maigrete at the Moët-Chandon château in Epernay, France.

I had a wonderful time—such a wonderful time, in fact, that I did not realize until several hours after the meal that the service had been totally formal. Beautiful platters of epicurean food had appeared as if by magic, and my wine glass seemed to remain forever filled. By the same magic, my empty plate was removed as soon as I had finished each course.

Fine silver and crystal sparkled by candlelight; there was the fragrance of fresh flowers; my table companions were witty—and, what's more, I felt that I was at my best. How did it happen? There were servants, many servants, yet I was never aware of their presence. I was only aware of the fact that I never lacked for anything at any time during the meal. It was all so beautiful, so festive. There was just enough of each delicious course. I ate but I didn't overeat. I drank but didn't drink too much. I felt great. It truly was fun.

Back home, I tried to analyze why and how the entire evening flowed so well. The dictionary defines formal as stiff, stilted, and solemn, but this party was none of those negative things. It was traditional, in that each thing was done as it had been done for many years in the past. However, ceremony was not "put on" for ceremony's sake but because it made for totally relaxed, leisurely, enjoyable dining. And that is the only reason this custom of good manners should exist.

I can manage to give only one or two formal dinner parties each year, and quite frankly I cheat a bit. I simply can't afford the necessary staff to do everything "according to Hoyle" so my parties are never strictly formal. But I do give my guests as much service as possible, and they love it and I love it too.

Nothing can make you feel more glamorous than presiding over a beautifully served dinner with your guests in full evening regalia—even though you have cooked the entire meal and set the table yourself. Why not try it? It's not all that difficult. Extra equipment can be rented and skilled help engaged for the occasion.

I will admit that there are more than a few rules to formal dining but remember that, like a complicated recipe, once you've done it, it's easy.

FORMAL DINNER PARTY RULES AND HOW TO BREAK THEM

Here is how to go about it—correctly—with some notes on how I break from tradition yet still give my guests an elegant evening—the feeling that this is a very special occasion created because they are very special people.

First you must decide the date and the size of the party and whom you are going to invite. Then get the invitations out early; three weeks ahead is not too premature and you should always allow at least two weeks. This way you can be more certain that the people you really want to come will be available for that particular evening.

Formal-dinner-party invitations must be written. They can be written entirely by hand or you can use those partially engraved cards that leave room for the guest's name, the type of party, and the date. These are frankly expensive (your name and address must be engraved on them), and unless you do a great deal of formal entertaining, I personally think they are a bit extravagant.

The invitations, whether engraved or handwritten, must be white or cream-colored cards of fairly stiff stock, about 4½ by 5½ inches, with their own matching envelopes. The form of invitations always follows this pattern:

Mr. and Mrs. John Henry Williams
request the pleasure of
Mr. and Mrs. Loving's
company at dinner
on Wednesday the tenth of April
at eight o'clock
15 Northeast Circle

R.S.V.P.
Black Tie

On engraved invitations, the only handwriting is the name of the guest, the occasion (dinner in this case), the date, and the time. Black ink is always used for handwriting on invitations.

I must admit that when sending this type of invitation to old and dear friends, I usually stick in a small note (on a separate piece of paper) to relieve the stiffness. Something like: "Dear Alex, Do come all gussied up. We're going to go all out—I hope!"

ABOUT HELP

You can and should select the menu, cook the meal, and set the table—or the evening will end up "a catered affair" and just as impersonal. You cannot, however, give a formal dinner party for even as few as four people without a minimum of two skilled helpers—a man to serve and a "backup" person in the kitchen who is skilled in food preparation.

Six to eight people require an extra server, and if you are having as many as twelve, a third server has to be engaged. Few hostesses can cope with more than twelve, so dinner parties beyond this size are not recommended in private houses. Actually, the pleasantest number is six or eight which can be beautifully served by a butler and waitress with help in the kitchen.

Few people today employ a full-time butler and waitress, but such help can usually be engaged from a catering service, or in smaller communities, there often are people in the area who make a profession of serving parties. In my own adopted Charleston, South Carolina, people would hardly think of giving an important party without "Mr. Izzac" or "Charles." First you call and secure their services—their availability sets the date—and you had better call well ahead of time.

If the people who are going to help you are "regulars" and have served in your house before, it is only necessary to have a dress rehearsal the afternoon of the party. If they are strangers, however, plan to have them come in one evening and serve a family meal in formal fashion to make certain of their skill and knowledge.

This all sounds a bit formidable but it is mandatory if you want to give a formal dinner. Nothing is more disappointing than to attempt one and then have it ruined by inept or incorrect service.

PARTY PROTOCOL

Now to start at the beginning . . . The butler opens the door and takes the guest's coats. The hostess greets them in the living room; she never opens the door herself. (This is the first rule I break. Mr. Izzac is too busy back in the kitchen preparing the serving platters and opening the wine.)

Cocktails or aperitifs are passed by the waitress along with some very simple hors d'oeuvres—cheese straws, salted almonds, and the like. (I sometimes have hors d'oeuvres already out on a side table and pass them myself.) No more than two cocktails are served before dinner so plan your timing accordingly. Traditionally guests are invited for eight o'clock and dinner is served at eight thirty. Guests are never asked before seven thirty and never after eight thirty.

If the first course is to be soup or oysters, it is on the table when guests enter the dining room. The soup plates are never more than three-fourths filled and are on their own service plate, and each is on top of the usually elaborate place plate. The napkins are folded and placed to the left of the forks.

If the first course is to be fish or perhaps a cold vegetable, the place plates only are on the table when guests are seated. Napkins are in position folded on the place plates. The guest removes the napkin and the place plate is removed and immediately replaced with a fish plate. The butler then offers the first course to each guest. This is presented in a serving dish or platter with serving fork and spoon in place, their handles toward the guest. The butler serves the guest from the guest's left side. He holds platters or serving dishes in the palm of his left hand, never by the rim. However, the server may steady the dish with his right hand. If the dish is hot, a folded napkin is placed under it to protect the server's hand.

The waitress immediately follows the butler with any accompanying sauce. As soon as the guests are served, the butler pours the wine and the waitress offers melba toast or crackers. (I sometimes have only Mr. Izzac to serve. In this case I try to eliminate a separate sauce.)

As soon as the diners have finished the first course, the plates are removed and immediately replaced by dinner plates. (The clearing away of dishes, by the way, is always done from the diner's right side.) If the first course was soup or oysters, the place plates are removed simultaneously at this time. The butler then serves the main course and is followed by the waitress with vegetables and/or rice or potatoes. (Or Mr. Izzac does both.) The butler refills the wine glasses—if there is only one wine such as champagne to be served. If a white wine was served with the first course and a different wine is planned for the main course, the glasses for the former are not removed. The butler simply pours the wine to accompany the main course into a second glass at each plate. If rolls are to be served, they are then passed, unbuttered, by the waitress. (I never serve them.) Butter is never served at a formal dinner.

If a separate fish course is to be served after the first course, the procedure is exactly the same, except that fish plates replace the first-course service. The wine is usually the same as that for the first course so the glasses are simply refilled. After the fish course, the dinner proceeds as outlined above.

Salads are always served separately; the dinner plate is removed and is replaced by the salad plate. The butler then serves the salad from a large bowl or tray. If the dressing is served separately, the waitress presents it and then serves crackers or toast. If the salad is to be accompanied by cheese, the butler passes the cheese tray and refills the wine glasses.

For the dessert, the table is completely cleared of plates, salt, pepper, and bread containers. The table is then crumbed by the waitress using a folded napkin to brush crumbs onto a small silver tray (large pieces of bread are removed first). Place cards are removed at the same time. If menu cards have been used, they too are removed with the salts and peppers. This is the only time during a formal meal that a diner's place is empty except for wine glasses which remain on the table.

The dessert service is then placed in front of each guest. This includes the dessert plate, finger-bowl doily, finger bowl (half filled with water), and dessert spoon and fork. The fork goes to the left, spoon to the right, on each side of the finger bowl. The guest removes the finger bowl and doily to the upper left of the dessert service. The dessert is then served by the butler; the waitress follows with any accompanying sauces or cookies. (When there is just Mr. Izzac to serve, I eliminate sauce or cookies.) The butler then pours the dessert wine if any is served. (If champagne was served with the main course, this is also my dessert wine. Otherwise, I do not serve one.)

Cigarettes may be offered by the butler just after he completes the dessert service. Traditionally, cigarettes are not offered at a formal meal, but modern custom makes it permissible to smoke after the salad course and, if preferred, cigarettes may be placed across a small ash tray with a folder of matches at each place. (If someone decides to "light up" during the main course, I couldn't care less.)

AFTER DINNER COFFEE

Coffee is always served in the living room and is offered by the butler. The coffee service is situated on a nearby table; the butler then places the coffeepot, sugar container, and spoon, a single small coffee cup, saucer, and coffee spoon on a small tray. Then, offering coffee to the women guests first, he says, "Coffee, madam?" He pours the one cup and hands it to the guest. The guest adds the desired amount of sugar, and the butler proceeds to the next guest. If the party consists of more than six people, the waitress will perform the same service using a second coffeepot, tray, and sugar container; otherwise service would be unpleasantly slow. If the party is small, the waitress accompanies the butler with a tray of additional cups, saucers, and spoons. (I usually have the coffee service brought in and then serve it myself as Mr. Izzac wants to finish up in the kitchen and go home.)

The butler follows the coffee service with a tray of any desired liqueurs or cognac. When the evening is over, guests say good night in the living room and the waitress helps them with their coats. The butler opens the door and says, "Good night, sir (or madam)." (I always do this myself.)

SETTING YOUR TABLE

At a formal dinner, not only does the service have a definite ritual, but the table setting must also follow a distinct pattern. Imaginative touches may lend wit and charm, but it is far better to be safe than sorry and in this case it's awfully easy to be sorry. The table may be covered with a cloth or left bare, but if a cloth is used, it is always plain white or ecru damask or linen, never lace. There are beautiful, delicately embroidered cloths to be had but they must be of really fine quality, and the embroidery should always be the color of the cloth. Brightly colored or flowered cloths are not used. Dinner napkins are large, usually 20-inch squares, and are always folded simply, never made into fancy shapes. If a bare table is preferred, the napkins should be extra handsome but never "cute."

It is not necessary or even desirable to have matching china for each course, but the dinnerware must be china, never earthenware or pottery. If you are lucky enough to have them, silver or vermeil (gold-plated silver) place plates are always good-looking. Quite presentable china can usually be rented, but it's nice to vary the monotony by using your own collection of antique plates, if you have them, for the salad or place plates.

The place plates, which set the tone of your decor, may be as elaborate as you like (within the bounds of good taste), and your color scheme must relate to them as well as to the plates that follow. But nothing need be a rigid match. For example, a Crown Derby place plate may have a rim of soft green bordered in gold, while the fish plates are lovely old painted Victorian antiques in muted colors. The dinner and salad plates may then be a particularly pretty Minton design of delicate red and pink with a tracing of green. To decorate the table you could use four tall silver candlesticks with two low silver bowls of mixed small roses, talisman, yellow, red, and pink with their own green leaves.

Or if the china is to be the usual gold-banded rentable variety, you can break up the routine by having the first course served on glass plates. These do not have to be expensive and they do give a lift to what might otherwise be a dull table. With this type of china, use crystal candlesticks, a bare table, and gleaming damask napkins. Don't try to brighten things up with color; play up the simple sophistication of white, gold, and crystal. Use all white flowers, tulips, roses, gardenias (especially effective when floated in a low crystal container) for maximum effect.

Centerpieces are rather simple. If you own a particularly handsome antique tureen or bowl, this can serve as a centerpiece without flowers, but there are usually understated flower arrangements on the formal table. Two smaller containers, each flanked by a pair of candles, are pretty on a table for six or eight. Tables of twelve require at least three arrangements, each with a pair of candlesticks.

Just keep in mind that the table should be not only simply elegant, but elegantly simple as well.

The actual setting of the table is again governed by a set of unbreakable rules as inflexible as those of service. The table is set first with the place plate as described above. Silver is placed in order of usage—the soup spoon to the far right, the fish knife (if there is a fish course) to the left of the soup spoon, and the dinner knife closest to the plate. Forks are placed on the left with fish fork to the far left, the dinner fork next, salad fork closest to the plate.

Place cards are centered just above the service plate and must be plain white, never colored or decorated. Individual salts and peppers are placed just above the dinner fork. Menu cards, if used, are just to the left of the tines of the fish fork. (I never use them.) Water and wineglasses are on the right, the water glass at the tip of the dinner knife, with the red-wine glass to the right, the white-wine glass slightly below the red. Napkins are placed directly on the service plate or to the left of the forks as described above. Wine bottles and wine coolers are always on a side table, never on the dinner table itself.

FORMAL MENUS

One final note: Plan your formal-dinner-party menu with care. There are six dinners included here, but you may want to change or vary them. Just keep in mind that formal dinner food is never robust and hearty. You may make the world's most delicious Beef Bourguignon or baked beans or apple pie but save them for a marvelous buffet. The same goes for thick soups, spareribs, fried chicken—any type of country or "peasant" food. It is delicious, but it is all wrong for a formal dinner. Years ago, formal dinners had as many as eight courses, but today soup, fish, main course, salad, and dessert are ample. Even the fish course is often dropped or used as a first course with soup omitted.

And there you have it. Really, when you think it through, giving a formal dinner is not all that overwhelming. Just remember that there is a reason for everything done at a formal dinner and that reason is to give your guests a good time.

So relax and enjoy it. If one or two things go wrong, no matter. Very few people will notice and besides, keep in mind that you are, after all, among friends—or you should be if you have followed the first rule in this book. Never invite anyone you don't like to your parties. A party is only a gift you give of your time and talent.

○

FORMAL DINNER: SPRING
(SERVES EIGHT)

Crabmeat Florentine

Chicken Breasts à l'Anglaise

Broccoli Ring with Fresh Peas, Tiny White Onions, and Pimentos

Watercress and Bibb Lettuce Salad with Crouton Dressing

Brie

Strawberries au Kirsch

Pecan Wafers

WINE: *White Burgundy Meursault, lightly chilled*

○

CRABMEAT FLORENTINE

2 packages (10-ounce size) frozen chopped spinach
3 tablespoons butter
1 tablespoon minced onions
1 teaspoon lemon juice
½ teaspoon salt
2 tablespoons flour
1½ cups milk
¼ cup dry sherry
¼ cup grated Swiss cheese
Salt
Pepper
Dash of Worcestershire sauce
1 pound crabmeat, fresh or frozen
1 cup fine dry bread crumbs
Butter slivers

Open packages of frozen spinach, place on a plate, and let stand at room temperature until thawed. This takes from 3 to 4 hours. Drain and press out water.

Heat 1 tablespoon of the butter in a small skillet. Add the onion and cook, stirring, for 1 minute. Add thawed spinach, salt, and lemon juice. Cover and cook for 1 to 2 minutes, only until spinach is hot. Remove from heat and spoon into 8 individual ramekins or other small shallow baking dishes. Flatten spinach out to cover bottom of dishes completely.

Melt remaining butter in a saucepan. Add flour and stir over low heat for 4 to 5 minutes. Slowly add milk, stirring as it is added. Cook over low heat until mixture thickens. Add sherry and cheese. Stir until cheese melts. Season with salt, pepper, and Worcestershire sauce. Remove from heat and add crabmeat. Spoon over spinach in ramekins. Sprinkle surface of each with bread crumbs. Dot with butter slivers.

NOTE: Recipe can be made ahead to this point. Cover each ramekin with plastic wrap and refrigerate until about one hour before serving.

Preheat oven to 350° F. and bake ramekins until thoroughly heated, about 20 minutes.

Place under direct broiler heat until tops are lightly browned.

⊙

CHICKEN BREASTS A L'ANGLAISE

4 chicken breasts
1 cup calvados
4 eggs
2 tablespoons water
3 cups fine dry bread crumbs
1 teaspoon salt
½ pound butter
1 cup corn or safflower oil
Thin slices of lemon
Sprigs of watercress

Have the butcher bone the chicken breasts, split them in half, and flatten them slightly with a cleaver.

Place breasts side by side in a single layer in a long shallow pan and sprinkle ½ cup of the calvados over them. Let stand at room temperature for about 30 minutes.

Beat the eggs with the water in a shallow bowl. Spread the bread crumbs out on waxed paper and sprinkle with salt.

Dip the chicken breasts in the egg mixture. Roll them in the bread crumbs. Cover completely with crumbs, then shake off excess crumbs.

NOTE: Recipe can be prepared ahead to this point. Refrigerate until ready to continue.

Melt ¼ pound of the butter and ½ cup of the oil in a large heavy skillet over medium heat. Add two of the chicken breasts and brown them lightly on both sides. Transfer to a long shallow baking dish. Repeat until all breasts have been browned. Add more butter and oil to the skillet as needed, reserving 2 tablespoons of the butter.

Pour the cooking oil and butter from the skillet. Add the reserved butter and melt over low heat. Add the remaining calvados. Pour about ½ of the mixture over the chicken breasts in baking dish. Place dish in a preheated 350° F. oven and bake for 25 to 30 minutes, basting with the remaining butter and calvados frequently.

Arrange breasts on serving platter and top each with a thin slice of lemon. Garnish with the sprigs of watercress.

⊙

BROCCOLI RING WITH FRESH GREEN PEAS, TINY WHITE ONIONS, AND PIMENTOS

The green peas and onions may be prepared a day ahead if desired. Reheat just before spooning into broccoli ring.

2 packages (10-ounce size) frozen chopped broccoli
2 tablespoons butter
2 tablespoons flour
1 cup light cream
¼ cup grated Swiss cheese
½ teaspoon salt
5 eggs, well beaten
½ cup fine cracker crumbs
Fresh peas, onions, and pimento (recipe below)

Preheat oven to 350° F.

Cook broccoli according to package directions. Drain thoroughly. Place on a wooden chopping board and chop very fine.

Melt the butter in a heavy saucepan and stir in the flour. Slowly add the cream, stirring as it is added. Cook, stirring often until mixture thickens. Add cheese and stir until melted. Season with salt. Remove from heat and cool slightly; then add the well-beaten eggs, beating with a wire whisk as they are added.

Stir in cracker crumbs and chopped broccoli.

Pour the mixture into a well-buttered ring mold. Place the mold in a larger pan and pour in sufficient warm water to extend halfway up the sides of the mold.

Bake in the preheated oven until firm, about 45 minutes. Unmold onto serving plate and fill center with peas, onions, and pimentos (recipe below).

FRESH GREEN PEAS, TINY WHITE ONIONS, AND PIMENTOS

8 tiny white onions, peeled
3 pounds fresh peas
½ teaspoon salt
2 tablespoons butter
½ cup water
½ cup chopped pimentos, well drained

In a saucepan, cover onions with water. Bring to boil and boil 3 minutes. Drain. Cover with fresh water. Place over low heat and let simmer until tender. Drain and set aside. This first 3-minute blanching assures a mild flavor.

Shell the peas and place them in a saucepan with the salt, butter, and water. Cover and cook over medium heat until tender, about 30 minutes. Add a little additional water if needed but no more than is necessary to keep bottom of pan covered with water.

When peas are almost tender, add boiled onions and pimentos. Continue to cook until onions are heated. Drain. Spoon mixture into center of broccoli mold.

⊙

WATERCRESS AND BIBB LETTUCE SALAD WITH CROUTON DRESSING

2 bunches watercress
3 heads Bibb lettuce
2 tablespoons lemon juice
4 tablespoons safflower or peanut oil
2 tablespoons honey
1 teaspoon fresh grated horseradish
¼ teaspoon salt
1 cup seasoned croutons

Wash and tear the watercress and lettuce into bite-size pieces, wrap loosely in very wet paper towels, and refrigerate until ready to assemble salad.

Have all dressing ingredients at room temperature. Combine lemon juice, oil, and honey in a small bowl and beat with a wire whisk until thick and well blended. Beat in horseradish and salt. Refrigerate, covered, until ready to serve.

A few minutes before serving time, place cress and lettuce in an attractive serving bowl and toss with dressing and croutons.

⊙

STRAWBERRIES AU KIRSCH

2 pints strawberries
½ cup sugar
½ cup Kirsch

Wash and hull berries. Cut berries in half and sprinkle them with sugar. Add Kirsch and toss to blend. Refrigerate 2 to 3 hours before serving.

⊙

PECAN WAFERS

½ cup (1 stick) butter, at room temperature
1½ cups brown sugar
¼ cup boiling water
2 eggs
¼ teaspoon salt
2 teaspoons baking powder
2 cups flour
½ cup chopped pecans

Cream the butter and brown sugar until well blended. Add the boiling water and beat until mixture is light and fluffy and all lumps have disappeared. Add the eggs and beat again until well blended.

Sift together the salt, baking powder, and flour and add them to the butter mixture, blending well. Stir in the pecans. Turn batter out on a lightly floured sheet of aluminum foil. Place, uncovered, in freezer until batter has stiffened enough to handle. Shape into a long, narrow roll. Wrap securely in foil and freeze until needed. When ready to bake, preheat oven to 350° F., slice off as many cookies as desired, and bake on a lightly buttered baking sheet for 10 to 15 minutes.

Makes about 36 cookies.

⊙

FORMAL DINNER: SUMMER
(SERVES EIGHT)

Cold Watercress Soup

Roast Fillet of Beef Slices with Sauce Aurora

Whole Roasted Baby Potatoes

Orange Shells Filled with Whipped Turnips

Sautéed Mushroom Caps

Cucumber and Spinach Salad

Peach Compote with Almonds

WINE: *Beaujolais Moulin-a-Vent*

○

COLD WATERCRESS SOUP

2 tablespoons butter
1 small onion, finely minced
6 cups chicken stock, fresh or canned
1 bunch watercress, finely chopped
2 cups light cream
Salt
White pepper
Watercress sprigs

Melt the butter in a large saucepan. Add minced onions and sauté over low heat until limp but not brown. Add chicken stock and chopped watercress, bring to a boil, and lower heat. Let simmer for 5 to 10 minutes. Remove from heat, stir in cream, and season to taste with salt and pepper. Chill for at least 3 hours. Serve very cold in chilled soup plates garnished with sprigs of watercress.

○

ROAST FILLET OF BEEF SLICES
WITH SAUCE AURORA

1 three and a half- to 4-pound fillet of beef, trimmed of skin and all surplus fat
2 tablespoons butter

Bring beef to room temperature. This is mandatory as the meat will not cook evenly if the center is even slightly chilled.

Bring butter to room temperature so that it is soft enough to spread on the meat.

Preheat oven to 500° F., allowing ample time for full heating.

Place the fillet on a rack in a roasting pan and fold narrow-end pieces under. Spread surface with soft butter.

Place the meat in the center of the oven and roast for 7

minutes at 500° F. Reduce oven temperature to 400° F. and continue to roast to desired degree of doneness. This first high heat seals in the juices; the lower temperature ensures that the center of the meat will be a juicy pink, rare but not raw.

Total roasting time for very rare: 20 minutes. For medium: a total of 30 minutes.

Let meat stand at room temperature for 15 to 30 minutes before slicing.

Slice and arrange in overlapping slices down the center of serving platter. Spoon Sauce Aurora (recipe below) down center of slices.

SAUCE AURORA
2 tablespoons butter
½ cup chopped shallots
4 tablespoons cognac or other good brandy
½ cup basic beef stock, fresh or canned
¾ cup heavy cream
¼ cup tomato puree
Salt
Pepper

Melt the butter in a heavy skillet. Add the shallots and sauté until limp but not browned. Add the cognac and cook, stirring over high heat, until reduced by half. Stir in the stock and let simmer until liquid is again reduced by half. Add the cream and stir until mixture is steamy hot. Do not allow to boil after adding cream. Remove from heat and stir in tomato puree. Season to taste with salt and pepper.

Makes about 1 cup of sauce.

NOTE: If substituting canned beef broth or stock for homemade, check for seasoning before adding salt. The commercially made varieties are almost always salty.

⊙

ORANGE SHELLS FILLED WITH WHIPPED TURNIPS

4 large thick-skinned oranges
10 small white turnips
1 tablespoon butter, at room temperature
1 teaspoon sugar
Salt
Freshly ground black pepper
Paprika

Cut oranges in half. Scoop out the pulp and reserve for another use.

Peel and dice turnips and place them in a saucepan. Add water to just cover. Bring to boil and let simmer until almost all water has been absorbed and the turnips are very tender. Remove from heat and mash until smooth. Stir in butter and sugar.

NOTE: Recipe can be made ahead to this point. Reheat before filling orange shells.

Season to taste with salt and pepper. Fill orange shells with mixture. Sprinkle with paprika.

May be kept warm in a 200° F. oven for up to 1 hour.

⊙

SAUTÉED MUSHROOM CAPS

16 large whole mushrooms
3 tablespoons butter
1 teaspoon lemon juice

Cut tough end of stems from mushrooms. Wash mushrooms under cold running water and pat dry on paper towels. Heat butter over medium flame. Add mushrooms and sauté until just tender, about 8 to 10 minutes. Sprinkle with lemon juice. Cover and keep warm until ready to serve. They can be reheated successfully at dinner time.

⊙

PEACH COMPOTE WITH ALMONDS

1½ cups sugar
1½ cups water
1 vanilla bean
8 large, firm but ripe peaches
½ cup cognac or other fine brandy
¼ cup slivered almonds

Combine the sugar, water, and vanilla bean in a saucepan. Bring to a boil and cook for 5 minutes. Remove from heat. Remove and discard vanilla bean. Plunge peaches in a large pan of boiling water for one minute. Drain and slip off skins. Cut in half and remove stones. Combine syrup with cognac in a large mixing bowl. Add peaches and almonds to syrup. Cover and refrigerate for at least 2 to 3 hours before serving.

NOTE: Compote may be prepared one day ahead if desired.

⊙

FORMAL DINNER: FALL
(SERVES EIGHT)

Château Consommé

Roast Fillet of Pork

Braised Endive

Orange Sweet Potatoes

Bibb and Boston Lettuce Salad

Camembert and Crackers

Frozen Soufflé Grand Marnier

Demitasse

Cognac

WINE: *Bordeaux St. Emilion*

☉

CHÂTEAU CONSOMMÉ

4 cups beef stock or consommé, fresh or canned
½ cup dry red wine
Salt
Pepper
2 truffles, thinly sliced

Combine stock and wine in a saucepan. Let simmer over low heat for 10 to 15 minutes. Season to taste with salt and pepper. Ladle into soup bowls. Float thin slices of truffle on each serving.

☉

ROAST FILLET OF PORK

3 pounds pork fillet
Salt
Pepper
8 tablespoons butter, at room temperature
½ cup melted butter
½ cup currant jelly
3 tablespoons soy sauce

Preheat oven to 450° F.

Have fillets at room temperature. Sprinkle meat with salt and pepper, spread with softened butter, and place in shallow roasting pan in preheated oven for 5 minutes. Lower heat to 350° F. and continue to roast for 30 minutes to the pound, basting occasionally with melted butter.

While the meat is roasting, melt the currant jelly in a small saucepan. Remove jelly from heat and blend in soy sauce. Baste meat with glaze during last 5 minutes of cooking.

Let fillets stand at least 20 minutes before carving into serving slices.

⊙

ORANGE SWEET POTATOES

3 pounds sweet potatoes
½ cup sugar
4 tablespoons butter
¼ teaspoon salt
½ cup orange juice
1 tablespoon grated orange peel
2 eggs, lightly beaten
½ cup heavy cream
¼ cup chopped walnuts

Preheat oven to 350° F.

Cook the sweet potatoes in boiling water until tender. Split; remove pulp to large mixing bowl. Add butter to hot potatoes and beat well. Add all remaining ingredients and beat until well blended. Pour mixture into a casserole.

NOTE: Potatoes may be prepared ahead to this point and stored, covered, in refrigerator until about 1 hour before serving. Bring to room temperature before proceeding to bake.

Bake in preheated oven for 20 to 30 minutes.

⊙

BRAISED ENDIVE

16 small endive
1 tablespoon salt
4 tablespoons tarragon vinegar
4 tablespoons butter, cut in slivers
1 cup beef or chicken stock, fresh or canned
Salt
Chopped parsley

Preheat oven to 350° F.

Remove loose and discolored leaves from endive. Trim the

heads and remove as much of the root as possible without cutting loose the leaves.

Fill a large pot with water. Add the tablespoon of salt and 2 tablespoons of the vinegar. Bring to a boil. Add the endive and let boil for 10 minutes. Drain.

Place endive, side by side, in a shallow baking dish.

Pour the remaining vinegar and the stock over them. Dot with the butter and sprinkle with salt. Cover loosely with foil. Place in the preheated oven and bake until tender, about 30 minutes.

Sprinkle with parsley immediately before serving.

NOTE: May be made ahead and reheated.

⊙

FROZEN SOUFFLÉ GRAND MARNIER

1 cup powdered sugar
6 egg yolks
3 cups heavy cream
1 tablespoon grated orange rind
¼ cup Grand Marnier
Preserved mandarin orange sections, drained

Combine the sugar and egg yolks in the top half of a double boiler over just simmering water. Beat with a wire whisk until the mixture is very fluffy and falls from the beater in a "ribbon." Remove from heat and continue to beat until mixture cools completely. Whip the cream until very stiff and fold into egg-sugar mixture. Add orange peel and Grand Marnier; fold in gently.

Tie a band of heavy paper around the top of a 1-quart soufflé mold to form a 2-inch-high collar. Pour the mixture into the mold and freeze, uncovered, until firm—at least 2 to 3 hours.

NOTE: Souffle may be prepared ahead and kept frozen for 2 or 3 days. In this case, wrap tightly in aluminum foil as soon as it has frozen.

To serve, remove paper collar and decorate with preserved mandarin orange sections. Let stand about 30 minutes before serving.

○

FORMAL DINNER: WINTER
(SERVES EIGHT)

Consommé Madrilene garnished with Curried Whipped Cream

Salmon Mousse with Caper Sauce Mousseline

WINE: *Puligny-Montrachet, lightly chilled*

Crown Roast of Lamb with Chestnut Puree

Fresh String Beans with Ribbon of Pimento

WINE: *Burgundy Côte de Nuits*

Bananas Parisian

Coffee

Cognac

○

CONSOMMÉ MADRILENE
WITH CURRIED WHIPPED CREAM

Make your own soup? Yes, certainly. It is infinitely better and far cheaper than the canned variety, and it is amazingly easy—the cooking time is long but you don't have to cook anything else along with it. Since the soup should barely simmer for hours, you can leave it unattended while you go about pleasanter things.

> 2 *pounds beef shank with bone left in*
> 2 *pounds veal bones*
> 5 *quarts water*
> 2 *teaspoons salt*
> 2 *teaspoons freshly ground black pepper*
> 6 *small onions, peeled and stuck with a clove*
> 2 *large leeks (optional)*
> 8 *sprigs parsley*
> 3 *carrots, scraped and cut in half*
> 4 *stalks celery, including leaves*
> 2 *bay leaves*
> 4 *tomatoes, cut in quarters*
> 2 *cups dry red wine*
> 4 *egg whites*
> 4 *eggshells*

Heat oven to 400° F.

Place the beef and bones in a deep, heavy kettle, 6- to 8-quart capacity (enamelized cast-iron is best). Place, uncovered, in preheated oven for 20 to 30 minutes, turning occasionally until veal bones and beef are evenly browned.

Remove meat and bones from oven and add all remaining ingredients except egg whites and shells. Bring to a rolling boil, skimming off any scum. Lower heat to a bare simmer—it should not bubble—and cook, uncovered, for 4 to 5 hours, or until bones are falling apart and marrow can be easily pushed out of the beef shanks. Cool to room temperature.

Remove meat, cover, and store in refrigerator or freezer for a separate meal. Remove and discard bones. Strain remaining liquid through a cheesecloth-lined colander into a smaller kettle. Refrigerate for 3 to 4 hours or until all fat has risen to the surface and congealed. Remove and discard congealed fat and bring stock to a brisk boil on top of the stove.

Meanwhile, beat the egg whites to a froth and crush the egg-shells. When the soup is boiling hard, pour in the whites and shells, bring to a boil again, stirring briskly. Remove from heat and pour through a cheesecloth-lined colander again into a refrigerator storage container.

Just before serving, heat to the boiling point, pour into consommé cups, and garnish with Curried Whipped Cream (recipe below). You don't absolutely *have* to clarify the soup but it does look prettier if you do.

Makes about 3 quarts of soup. You will need at least 2 quarts for the dinner, but the remainder can be refrigerated or frozen to use as stock for any number of dishes.

NOTE: This consommé may be served cold if desired; it jellies perfectly. If kept for more than 1 week, cover securely and store in freezer.

CURRIED WHIPPED CREAM
½ *pint whipping cream*
2 *teaspoons curry powder*
¼ *teaspoon salt*
2 *tablespoons slivered pistachio nuts*

Have cream bowl and wire whisk icy cold. Beat cream until very stiff, then fold in curry powder, salt, and pistachio nuts. Keep very cold until just before spooning on hot soup. Serve immediately.

⊙

HOT SALMON MOUSSE
WITH CAPER SAUCE MOUSSELINE

2 pounds fresh salmon, free of bones and skin
2 tablespoons minced parsley
6 egg whites
1½ cups heavy cream
2 teaspoons salt
2 teaspoons white pepper

Put the salmon through the finest blade of a food grinder, stir in the parsley. Divide the egg whites in half and pour 3 of them into salmon-parsley mixture. Blend very well, using a heavy wooden spoon. Chill for 1 hour.

Work the heavy cream in thoroughly. Blend in salt and pepper. Whip the remaining egg whites until they are stiff but not dry and fold into salmon. Pour into a 2-quart soufflé mold and cover with a piece of buttered brown (or parchment) paper. Place in a large pan of hot water deep enough for the water to come three-fourths of the way up the sides of the mold.

Bake in a preheated 350° F. oven for 25 to 30 minutes or until firm. The mousse may be kept in the pan of hot water until a few minutes before serving. If it is to be turned out on a tray, remove it from the hot water 8 to 10 minutes before turning out of mold.

Pass Caper Sauce Mousseline (recipe below) in a separate bowl.

CAPER SAUCE MOUSSELINE
1 cup butter
4 egg yolks
1 cup heavy cream
2 tablespoons lemon juice
½ teaspoon salt
1 tablespoon capers, drained

Melt the butter in the top half of a double boiler over very low heat. Let cool to room temperature. Beat the egg yolks with the cream until thick and well blended. Combine with the melted butter. Add lemon juice and salt. Blend well. Return to heat and cook over very low heat, beating constantly with a whisk until the sauce thickens. *Do not allow to boil.* Place over hot water at very low heat until ready to serve, beating occasionally with a whisk. Stir in capers just before serving.

Makes about 2½ cups of sauce.

○

CROWN ROAST OF LAMB

1 16-rib crown of lamb
Salt
Pepper
6 strips bacon
16 cubes raw potatoes
½ cup butter
1 clove garlic
3 tablespoons chopped parsley

Have your butcher tie the crown with string. Do not let him sew it together as you will want to remove the string and carve the roast before serving. He should also trim the bones evenly.

Preheat oven to 500° F.

Bring meat to room temperature and rub with salt and pepper. Wrap lower portion of the crown with strips of bacon, fastening them in place with cocktail picks. Stick a potato cube over each bone end to prevent burning. Place the crown on a rack in the preheated oven and sear for 15 minutes. Lower heat to 350° F. and continue to roast for 1½ to 2 hours.

While the meat is roasting, melt the butter in a small saucepan and add the garlic clove. Cook over very low heat for about 5 minutes.

Remove and discard the garlic and baste roast frequently with the garlic-flavored butter and the drippings in the roasting pan. When roast is done, remove potato cubes and bacon slices and discard.

Allow the roast to stand for 15 or 20 minutes after removing from heat, then carve into chops.

Fill the center of a serving platter with a mound of Chestnut Puree (recipe below), then reconstitute the chops into a crown

around the puree. Sprinkle with chopped parsley before serving.
If available, top each bone end with a paper frill.

CHESTNUT PUREE
3 pounds chestnuts
Milk, as needed
2 tablespoons butter, at room temperature
1 tablespoon sugar
Salt
Pepper

With a sharp knife, cut a slit on the convex side of each
chestnut. Place chestnuts in saucepan and cover with water. Bring
to a boil, lower heat, and let simmer for 10 minutes. Drain and
cool. Remove shells, and with a sharp knife, remove brown skins.

Return chestnuts to saucepan and add enough milk to cover.
Let simmer over low heat until tender, about 30 minutes. Drain
and mash. Add butter and sugar. Season to taste with salt and
pepper.

NOTE: Recipe may be made ahead to this point.
Reheat and keep warm in top of double boiler over simmering water.

⊙

BANANAS PARISIAN

8 ripe bananas
4 tablespoons lemon juice
1 cup apricot jam
¾ cup brown sugar
1 cup heavy cream
3 tablespoons confectioners sugar
6 tablespoons sour cream
2 tablespoons Kirsch
2 tablespoons slivered almonds

Peel and slice the bananas in half lengthwise. Dip in lemon
juice and place on a baking sheet. Spread each banana slice with
apricot jam, then sprinkle evenly with brown sugar. Place under
moderate broiler flame for 5 to 6 minutes until sugar is melted
and bananas are slightly softened. *Do not overcook.*

Transfer bananas to individual dessert dishes or to a large serving dish. Refrigerate until just ready to serve.

Whip the cream until very stiff. (Have cream, bowl, and wire whisk very cold.) Blend in sugar, sour cream, and Kirsch. Spread over bananas and sprinkle with almonds. Serve at once.

○

FORMAL DINNER: CHRISTMAS EVE
(SERVES EIGHT)

Oysters on the Half Shell with Lemon Wedges

Quail Smitane

Brussels Sprouts with Wild Rice

Watercress and Bibb Lettuce Salad

Mincemeat Tarts in Cream-cheese Pastry

Espresso with Cognac

WINE: *French Champagne*

○

QUAIL SMITANE

2 tablespoons butter
1 small white onion, finely chopped
1 cup mushrooms, finely chopped
1 cup dry bread crumbs
¼ cup dry vermouth
1 egg, lightly beaten
8 quail
Salt
Pepper
½ cup butter
¼ cup cognac
1 cup dry white wine
1 cup sour cream, at room temperature
2 tablespoons chopped parsley

Melt the 2 tablespoons of butter in a deep, heavy skillet. Add the onions and mushrooms and sauté until soft.

In a large mixing bowl, combine bread crumbs, sautéed onions and mushrooms, vermouth, and beaten egg. Mix well to blend. Stuff each quail lightly with this mixture and sew up the cavity. Rub each quail with salt and pepper.

Melt the ½ cup of butter in the skillet used to sauté the mushrooms and onions and brown each bird on all sides over medium heat. Transfer browned birds to a deep, flameproof casserole.

Warm the cognac slightly in a small saucepan, pour over birds, and ignite. When the flame subsides, pour in the white wine and cover the casserole tightly. Simmer over low heat for about 25 minutes or until birds are tender.

Just before serving, add the sour cream and heat over very low heat for 5 to 10 minutes. *Do not allow to boil.* Arrange birds on a serving platter and sprinkle with parsley.

Serve sauce separately.

⊙

BRUSSELS SPROUTS WITH WILD RICE

1 pound brussels sprouts
2 teaspoons salt
1 tablespoon lemon juice
1½ cups wild rice
1 teaspoon salt
4 cups boiling water
2 tablespoons butter

Wash the sprouts, discarding any discolored outer leaves. Cut off stems and cut gashes in the stem end. Soak the sprouts in ice-cold water with the 2 teaspoons of salt. Drain, then plunge into rapidly boiling water. Cook only until barely tender. Drain and immediately fill pot with cold water to stop the cooking process. Drain again and refrigerate until ready to use.

Wash the wild rice and add it with 1 teaspoon of salt to boiling water; lower heat and cook until tender, about 40 minutes. Drain well, add butter, and keep hot over very low flame. Chop brussels sprouts coarsely and add to rice. Cover and keep over low flame until sprouts are hot.

⊙

MINCEMEAT TARTS IN CREAM-CHEESE PASTRY

2 packages (3-ounce size) cream cheese, at room temperature
½ cup butter, at room temperature
1½ cups flour
2 cups mincemeat
2 tablespoons cognac

Mix cream cheese and butter. Add flour and work mixture with fingers until smooth. Chill well for at least 1 hour.

Preheat oven to 450° F.

Roll out pastry to ⅛-inch thickness. Fit into 8 individual tart pans. Combine mincemeat with cognac and blend well. Fill pastry with mincemeat mixture. Bake at 450° F. for 10 minutes, then reduce heat to 300° F. and bake an additional 25 minutes.

NOTE: If you have pastry left over after filling the tart pans, sprinkle it with grated cheese and paprika. Cut pastry into strips, twist gently, and bake at 450° F. for 10 minutes. Makes great cheese straws for cocktails or salad accompaniment.

⊙

FORMAL DINNER: NEW YEAR'S EVE
(SERVES EIGHT)

Consommé Velours
Rock Cornish Game Hens Madeira

Sherried Carrots

Sautéed Artichoke Hearts

Watercress Garnish

Pont-l'Évêque Cheese

Unsalted Crackers

Boules de Neige

Café Filtre with Cognac

WINE: *Champagne*

⊙

CONSOMMÉ VELOURS

2 *tablespoons butter*
8 *mushrooms, finely chopped*
2 *quarts chicken stock, fresh or canned*
⅓ *cup minute tapioca*
1 *egg yolk, lightly beaten*
½ *cup heavy cream*
½ *cup dry sherry*

Melt the butter in a deep saucepan. Add the mushrooms and sauté until soft but not brown. Add chicken stock and bring to a boil. Gradually add the tapioca, stirring constantly. Cook over medium heat for 10 minutes. Remove from heat. Mix 2 tablespoons of the hot soup into the beaten egg yolk. Add mixture slowly to soup, stirring constantly. Add cream and sherry and stir well to blend. Reheat to steamy hot but do not allow to boil.

NOTE: Soup may be prepared the day before and refrigerated, well covered, until about 1 hour before serving. Allow to come to room temperature before reheating over very low heat.

○

ROCK CORNISH GAME HENS MADEIRA

8 Rock Cornish hens
Salt
Pepper
2 tablespoons butter, at room temperature
1 cup chicken stock fresh or canned
¼ pound butter, melted
½ cup Madeira
1 tablespoon lemon juice
3 tablespoons currant jelly
1 beurre-manie (made by kneading 1 teaspoon flour into 2
  teaspoons soft butter)
8 kumquats, bottled in heavy syrup, drained and cut in half
  lengthwise
4 cups cooked wild rice
Sprigs of watercress

Preheat oven to 450° F.

Rub the hens inside and out with salt, pepper, and the 2 tablespoons of softened butter.

Place the birds, side by side, in a long, shallow pan that is just large enough to hold them closely together.

Place in the preheated oven and roast, uncovered, for 10 minutes. Reduce heat to 350° F. and continue to roast for 25 minutes, basting often with the stock and the ¼ pound of melted butter.

Remove the birds from the pan and keep them warm.

Pour the cooking liquid from the pan into a small saucepan. Place over moderate heat and cook until reduced to about ½ cup. Add the Madeira, lemon juice, and currant jelly. Stir until jelly has dissolved. Add the beurre-manie and continue to stir until the sauce is smooth.

Return the hens to the roasting pan and pour the sauce over them. Place in 350° F. oven and roast a final 10 minutes.

Gently stir the kumquat halves into the wild rice and mound the mixture on the center of the serving platter. Arrange the hens around the rice and garnish with sprigs of watercress. Serve the sauce separately.

⊙

SHERRIED CARROTS

2 pounds carrots
4 tablespoons butter
1 small white onion, quartered
3 tablespoons water
½ teaspoon salt
3 tablespoons sugar
½ cup sherry

Scrape the carrots under cold running water and cut them into bite-size pieces.

Melt the butter in a heavy saucepan. Add carrots, onion, water, and salt. Cover tightly and bring to a boil over high heat. Lower heat and continue to cook over medium heat for about 15 minutes or until carrots are almost tender. Uncover pan as little as possible during the first 15 minutes but shake occasionally to prevent burning.

Remove cover. Remove and discard onion. Add sugar and sherry and again bring to a boil. Cover, lower heat, and cook for an additional 10 minutes or until carrots are very tender and all liquid has been absorbed.

NOTE: Recipe may be made ahead and reheated.

⊙

SAUTÉED ARTICHOKE HEARTS

4 tablespoons butter
1 clove garlic, peeled
2 packages (10-ounce size) frozen artichoke hearts
3 tablespoons vermouth or dry white wine
½ teaspoon salt
2 tablespoons minced chives or parsley

Melt the butter in a heavy saucepan, one with a tight-fitting lid. Add the garlic clove and sauté for 1 minute over low heat. Remove and discard garlic.

Add artichoke hearts, vermouth, and salt. Cover and cook 5 to 10 minutes or until artichoke hearts are tender. Sprinkle with chives or parsley before serving.

NOTE: Recipe may be made ahead and reheated.

○

BOULES DE NEIGE
(ICE CREAM BALLS)

¼ cup candied cherries, finely chopped
¼ cup candied orange peel, finely chopped
¼ cup candied citron, finely chopped
¼ cup Kirsch
1 quart French vanilla ice cream
1 cup heavy cream
1 cup coconut
Candied violets (optional)

Combine the candied fruits with the Kirsch and marinate for at least 1 hour. Toss frequently to distribute the Kirsch.

Place the ice cream in a large mixing bowl and allow to soften slightly. Add fruit and Kirsch and blend to distribute evenly. Pack into either a spherical bombe mold or into any small, deep round metal bowl (in this case cover top tightly with aluminum foil) and freeze for at least 3 to 4 hours or until very firm.

Unmold the ice cream onto a serving plate and cover with cream; sprinkle heavily with coconut and decorate with candied violets. Refreeze until about 30 minutes before serving.

NOTE: Ice cream will unmold more easily if the mold is lightly greased with salad oil before filling.

About
Cooking
Ahead

⊙

You like your friends, you want to give them a good time, and you want to serve them really great food—but you also want to be with them at the party, not back in the kitchen cooking frantically. I feel the same way. Though I enjoy preparing the food (I find it the most creative part of giving a party), I want to go about it in a leisurely fashion, without last-minute panic. Long before the festivities begin, I plan a menu that can be prepared in easy stages and mostly made in advance—as I have planned all the menus in this book. Then I do part of the work two or three days—sometimes a week—ahead. I finish the remaining dishes that can be precooked one day before hand, and I do all other necessary cooking as early as possible on the day of the party.

With the exception of roasted meats, which are usually easy because they can be put in the oven just before you dress for the evening and after being cooked should stand at room temperature for about 30 minutes, this leaves only the quick tasks of reheating hot dishes and arranging cold foods on serving platters or plates. I do almost all this after I'm dressed for the party, in an easy 30 minutes before guests are due to arrive. The remainder, which is very little, I attend to after everyone—including me—has been served his first drink.

Some of the things you can do in advance of a party:

ONE WEEK AHEAD

Prepare any frozen dessert. Wrap airtight and store in freezer.

Bake and stuff potatoes (with butter, cheese, and seasoning; see recipe, page 28). Freeze on flat surface, then wrap individually in plastic sandwich bags, squeeze out air, seal, and store in freezer. Reheat, frozen, in covered dish in 350° F. oven. Reheating takes about 1 hour. They taste even better after a stay in the cold.

You can also prepare and freeze baked beans successfully. Undercook the beans by about 30 minutes. Wrap casserole completely in foil and freeze while still warm. Defrost completely before reheating; this takes from 4 to 6 hours at room temperature, depending on size of casserole.

TWO OR THREE DAYS AHEAD

Prepare any custard that is to be served cold. Transfer while hot to serving bowl (or individual bowls). Cover surface of custard directly with plastic wrap to keep film from forming. When custard is cool, wrap bowl in foil or plastic wrap. Store in refrigerator.

Prepare any meat or chicken dish that is made with ample sauce. Undercook recipe by about 20 minutes. Cover and store in refrigerator. Bring to room temperature before reheating.

ONE DAY AHEAD

Prepare any dessert. Cover or wrap in foil. Store in refrigerator. Fruit compotes, especially those made with liqueur, are at their best if made ahead so that flavors can mellow. Bring cakes or cookies to room temperature and reheat pies briefly in the oven before serving.

Split and butter—with room-temperature butter—rolls. Wrap loosely in foil. Store in refrigerator. Heat in same foil.

Boil, peel, and devein shrimp if they are to be served cold. Place in plastic wrap, squeeze out air, seal, and store in refrigerator.

EARLY ON THE DAY OF THE PARTY

Prepare any au-gratin seafood dish (creamed seafood topped with bread crumbs such as Coquilles of Crabmeat and Shrimp). Cover with foil. Store in refrigerator. Bring to room temperature before reheating.

Prepare any cream sauce or creamed dish in top half of double boiler. While still hot, cover sauce directly with plastic wrap. Cover pan and store in refrigerator. Place pan over, not in, simmering water to reheat. Stir often.

Prepare greens for salad or garnish. Wash thoroughly. Drain in colander, then wrap loosely in very wet (cold water) paper toweling. Store in vegetable bin of refrigerator—they will be crisper than when you bought them as well as bone dry—as all greens should be before being tossed with dressing. You can also prepare ahead any salad dressing.

Set up the bar.

TWO OR THREE HOURS BEFORE YOUR GUESTS ARRIVE

Prepare any vegetables. Cover and leave at room temperature. And you can boil rice—prepare as directed on package. Drain into a colander. Place colander over, not in, just simmering water. Cover colander with a clean kitchen towel that has been wrung out in hot water. When you are ready to serve it, this rice will be fluffy with each grain separate and beautifully dry.

FINAL NOTE: Look over your menu and decide on a cooking schedule that will leave you rested and fresh, ready for the party. Have fun.

About Drinks
Before Dinner

⊙

Even if I know my guests do not drink hard liquor, I still offer some kind of "cocktail"—usually lemon-spiked tomato juice with a "swizzle stick" of leafy celery, or a Bloodless Mary. I find the easiest way to break the ice and get the conversation off to a good start is: "Now that everyone knows each other, what would you like to drink?" Also, it's a good way to direct people to where you want them to sit: "John, will you take Elsa's drink out to the terrace for her?" Or: "I think you'll be comfortable over by the fireplace—you can put your drinks on the coffee table."

When people do drink—and almost everyone these days will accept at least a mild aperitif—remember that dinner parties are not cocktail parties so curtail the before-the-meal drinking or your guests will be too foggy to really enjoy the meal.

I never serve more than two drinks before a seated dinner, three for a serve-yourself-anytime buffet. Latecomers get short shrift, otherwise guests who have arrived on time will either over-imbibe or stand around with empty glasses. Serious drinkers can go back to serious drinking after dinner, but too many drinks beforehand will only spoil the evening for everyone else.

If I know my guests enjoy fine wine, I offer a wine-based aperitif or champagne as the cocktail. Hard liquor before wine does dull its appreciation. Some people simply can't relax without at least one stiff drink, however, so I always offer a choice. Scotch, blended whiskey, vodka, gin, or bourbon on the rocks or with water or soda. I also have orange juice and a Bloody Mary mix available. But I never get involved with complicated mixed concoctions like Manhattans or Pink Ladies as they usually spoil the appetite for both food and wine to follow.

SETTING UP THE BAR

As to the actual serving . . . Set up your bar before your guests arrive. I've given several suggestions on how to do this in each section, but I'll remind you here to decide ahead of time on the routine of both making and serving the drinks. This is traditionally the host's responsibility, but the host may appoint a friend or a hostess may ask a male guest to "do the honors."

At a large card-table or buffet party, set up the bar as far away from the food as possible; this avoids traffic jams. And after serving the first drinks, suggest that the male guests make their own and serve the ladies. For a very large party, you can of course engage a bartender, but unless you are really having a crowd I don't think this is necessary.

To stock your bar you will need:

Bottle opener
Corkscrew
Set of ice tongs
Large mixing pitcher
Jigger
Long-handled mixing spoon
Coasters
Stirrers
Napkins
Old-Fashioned glasses
Stainless-steel knife
Ice bucket
Serving tray
Cocktail glasses
Champagne glasses
Highball glasses

HOW MUCH LIQUOR SHOULD YOU BUY?

One fifth-size bottle (four-fifths of a quart) of liquor makes 17 of any of these drinks, using 1½ ounces per drink.

Highballs
Whiskey Sours
Martinis
Gin and Tonics
Whiskey on the Rocks
Old-Fashioneds
Gin on the Rocks

IF YOU'RE HAVING	FOR PRE-DINNER COCKTAILS YOU'LL AVERAGE
4 people	8 to 12 drinks *(one fifth required)*
6 to 8 people	12 to 24 drinks *(two fifths required)*
12 people	24 to 36 drinks *(three fifths required)*
20 people	40 to 60 drinks *(four fifths required)*
25 people	50 to 75 drinks *(five fifths required)*
40 people	80 to 120 drinks *(eight fifths required)*

About Wine

⊙

Should you serve wine?

I usually do; to me it is the perfect beverage for most meals after eleven o'clock in the morning unless the menu demands another beverage.

Have you ever had a glass of champagne with a festive brunch? Lovely! Or sipped Chianti with your twelve o'clock hamburger? Just try it. A good wine enhances the pleasure of almost all food, and most people truly enjoy it with dinner.

There is no need to make a "production" about buying, serving, or drinking wine. If in doubt about what to buy, consult an expert. Steer clear of your corner liquor store; the owner more often than not knows less than you do. Instead seek out the best, most reliable wine merchant in your town. Give him your menu and tell him your budget. Then rely on his selection. Lacking professional help, however, any wine you have discovered on your own and like is a good wine to serve at your party.

Nonetheless, generations and generations of gourmets, wine lovers, and wine experts, each with his individual and sometimes unorthodox taste, have agreed that there are certain "marriages" of food and wine which are pleasant to everybody.

The following marriages are among those which meet with general approval. When uncertain it is best to go along with them:

HORS D'OEUVRES: *light dry white wine, dry sherry, rosé, dry champagne*

FISH: *dry white wine, rosé, dry champagne*

WHITE MEAT AND POULTRY: *dry white wine, light red wine, rosé, dry champagne*

RED MEAT AND GAME: *full-bodied red wine*

CHEESE: *red wine with pungent cheeses; otherwise, any good dry wine*

DESSERT: *dry champagne, semisweet champagne, sauterne, or other semisweet or sweet dessert wines*

WITH OR AFTER COFFEE: *fortified wines such as cognac or brandy, sweet or dry sherry*

UNCORKING

Red wine is improved if the bottle is uncorked about an hour before the meal. It is dormant in the bottle, and as soon as the bottle is uncorked, the wine is "awakened" and starts "breathing." It absorbs oxygen from the air, and this oxidation activates the development of the "bouquet" and the aroma. One hour or so of "breathing" gives depth and smoothness to red wine.

White and rosé wines have a very delicate fragrance. They would lose their freshness if they were exposed to the air for too long a time. Therefore, these bottles should be opened just before serving.

Champagne, of course, is also served as soon as it is opened.

GLASSES

The use of many different types of wine glasses is fortunately becoming obsolete as it is completely unnecessary.

All experts agree that one type of wine glass is perfect for all wines, including champagne. The perfect glass is long-stemmed and tulip-shaped with a bowl the size of an orange. It is clear and thin, without heavy ornamentation. As a matter of fact, any large glass or goblet is better than a small, so-called wine glass.

SERVING

Wine is poured as soon as food is brought to the table. It is the host or the butler, rather than the hostess or waitress, who serves the wine and sees to it that glasses are replenished during the meal.

Wine glasses are never filled to brimming but instead are poured half-full. The reason for this is to allow space for the "bouquet" that is part of the pleasure of drinking wine.

One standard-size bottle of wine (a fifth) contains about four servings, so for four people I plan on having two bottles of wine.

Incidentally, wine does not necessarily have to be expensive to be good. Experiment a little on your own before the party. I once discovered a Spanish burgundy for a little less than a dollar a bottle that was superb. You may not be that lucky, but it does pay to try a few lesser-known wines. If you are unsure yourself, ask a friend who is a more practiced connoisseur to a "tasting" for his opinion.

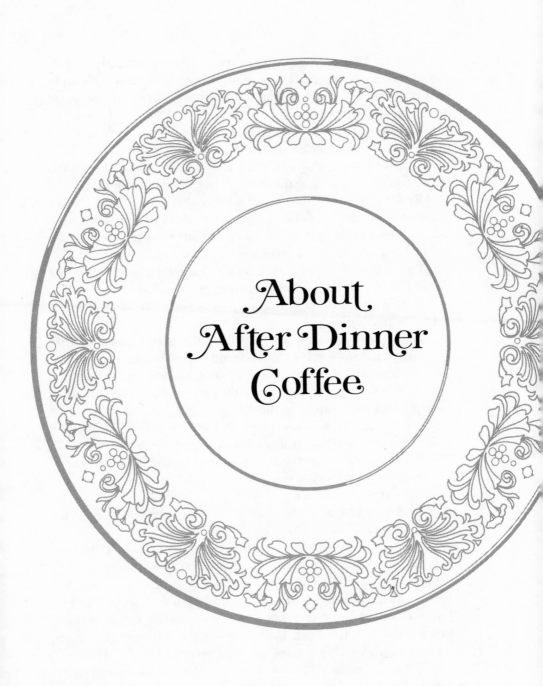

About
After Dinner
Coffee

○

Occasionally I have guests at my dinner table who really want a cup of coffee with their dessert. If I know this—unless it's a truly formal dinner—I bring in the coffee service. After all, the party is for their enjoyment.

Nevertheless, I usually prefer to serve coffee after dessert and in the living room. There are two reasons for this: first, it gives people something to do right after the meal, and second, it starts the conversation going again after people have left the table.

Really well made, hot, and fragrant coffee served from a silver (or silverplate) pot in delicate demitasse cups can transform even the simplest dinner into an occasion. Yet such coffee can be easily made ahead and kept hot until time to serve.

I use a glass drip pot—the kind that makes use of a filter paper —and I follow all the rules for making great coffee:

Start with a thoroughly clean pot. Rinse with hot water just before beginning.

Fresh coffee is always best. Buy freshly roasted beans and grind them in your own electric coffee grinder just before brewing, or buy the best quality vacuum-packed coffee and use it within one week after opening the can. (Once the can has been opened, cover with plastic top and store in the refrigerator.)

Fresh water is important too. For superb coffee, use bottled water or let tap water run until very cold.

For best results, use the full capacity of your coffee maker.

For lesser quantities, use a smaller coffee maker. Never brew less coffee than ¾ of the coffee maker's capacity.

Coffee should never be boiled. When coffee is boiled, it becomes bitter and oily.

To make coffee ahead, I prefer to use the following method:

As soon as the coffee is brewed (obviously not in an electric coffee maker) place pot in a pan containing sufficient hot but not boiling water to come halfway up sides of pot. Keep water hot, but not boiling, over very low heat. Immediately before serving, bring water to a full boil. Rinse serving pot out with hot water. Transfer coffee to hot serving pot and serve at once.

To make eight demitasse servings of medium-strong coffee, use the following ratio of coffee to water: 4 cups of water to 4 level tablespoons of coffee

Naturally cream is never used in demitasse cups, but sugar may be. If you prefer lump sugar, make it the tiny dot size, and for a bit of color and flavor add a small thin twist of lemon peel.

FOR TRUE CAFÉ ESPRESSO

Buy an authentic Italian espresso machine; prepare it ready to brew. Then brew just before serving. Just make sure you like espresso, however, before buying, as these machines are expensive.

COFFEE WITH LIQUEURS

CAFÉ ROYALE: Place a lump of sugar into a demitasse cup that is half full of very strong coffee and slowly fill the cup with cognac or a good brandy. If this is done carefully, off the back of a spoon, the brandy will stay on top. Light the brandy and when you are quite drunk with the beauty of the blue flame, quench it with spooned coffee.

CAFÉ COINTREAU: Place 1 demitasse spoon of grated lemon peel into demitasse cup, fill ⅔ full with coffee. Fill to brim with Cointreau. Stir.

ITALIAN COFFEE: A drip pot may be used but a *macchenetta* (Italian-style drip pot) is best. Use Italian dark roast coffee and follow manufacturer's directions.

IRISH COFFEE

Serve Irish Coffee instead of dessert.

Rinse out heavy-stemmed water goblets with hot water. Dry thoroughly. Fill to about 2 inches below the rim with freshly brewed strong coffee. Add 2 teaspoons sugar and 1 jigger of Irish whiskey. Stir once, then top with a heaping tablespoon of lightly whipped heavy cream. Do not stir but sip the hot coffee through the cool cream.

About
How to Turn
the Party On

⊙

It's been said that it takes people to turn a party on, interesting people, with wit, charm and gaiety. But to my way of thinking it's more the other way around. Turn the party on and ordinary garden- and office-variety people like me, and maybe like you, *become* interesting, witty, charming, and gay.

How do you turn a party on? Make it a smashing success? Bring everyone up to a "special" mood and give them a really great time? Even if you are a shy, quiet, and reserved type of person it's easy—if you know how. Here is the formula and it works for every party from a small informal gathering to what I call a real bash.

The secret is party decoration—all through the house, inside and out; party lighting; party food and drink, the very best and plenty of it; party tables, festive, special, different from every day; party music, with never a raucous note. And *you*—in a party mood, honestly glad to see your friends.

PARTY DECORATIONS

People are affected by their surroundings to a much greater degree than you might think. Obviously a dingy, unattractive house or apartment is not conducive to a party mood, but neither is one that has no genuine warmth no matter how well decorated, how elegant, or how grand.

Start your party atmosphere outside. Does your front door say welcome? Is the entranceway clean and well lighted? Why not have a big basket of flowers at the doorway, or a bouquet of festive balloons? I remember one especially happy party where the hostess had the front door flanked by masses of flowering plants, and there was a marvelous musician playing an accordion to usher us into the house. First impressions such as these—lights, flowers, color, music—break the ice, make people start talking, and make the party click right from the start.

Party houses should be clean; nothing looks drearier than a dingy setting. Floors must shine, bathrooms must sparkle, and the whole house must smell wonderfully fragrant. I always take time to give every room a thorough cleaning before any party. Then and only then do I add the extra-special touches that create a festive air.

Flowers especially quicken the senses, making people come alive. I like small bouquets all over the house, even in the powder room and, if it's an informal evening, I usually have a big stoneware jar of daisies or other "country" flowers in my kitchen.

PARTY LIGHTING COMES NEXT

Display directors of big stores and stage-set people will tell you that lighting alone can do more to create a mood than anything else. First rule: no overhead lighting at all. Direct ceiling lights make everyone look tired and older; use lamps instead. I like to use colored bulbs, pale pink for a rosy glow or, in certain rooms, pale yellow. Buy a supply of light bulbs a few days before your party and try them out. You'll be amazed at the difference this change of light color can make.

The best party lighting, in my opinion, is a combination of candles and lamps. There is something about the glow of candlelight that puts people in a mellow, relaxed frame of mind. I usually have candles on the mantlepiece, on the coffee table, and on small side tables as well as on the dinner table.

Outside lighting is important too. Not only should your entranceway be well lighted but, if you have a garden or terrace, why not light these also? I use candles in holders with small hurricane shades that stand on tall iron poles. You stick them in the ground and they look lovely. I sometimes string a chain of electric lights in the garden and cover them with Japanese lanterns. Light up the night and you light up the party.

PARTY FOOD AND DRINK

Regardless of whether the party is as simple as having a few friends over for an informal buffet or as elaborate as a formal dinner, the food and drink should be topnotch. I've given all types of parties for all kinds of people, and let me assure you that when the food is good, everyone is happy, including the hostess and host.

PARTY TABLES

Throughout this book I have made suggestions for table settings and hopefully you will find them useful. But, like any other work of art, a table setting should reflect your personality and that of your house. Create excitement with color, texture, pattern, and shape. Express yourself—go all out if you like—but remember that people must be served, or serve themselves, easily, in a relaxed manner to truly enjoy the food.

PARTY MUSIC

Music unquestionably turns people on. It need not be anything more than carefully selected records on the hi-fi, but do stick to popular "everybody likes it" kinds of tunes. As much as you might enjoy opera or hard rock, these are not always someone else's cup of tea. Safe bets are Cole Porter or Rodgers and Hammerstein—that type of thing—but do keep it low. And no vocals please; they distract from conversation.

For a really gala party, it's fun to hire a pianist or an accordionist for the evening—or even a trio of musicians. Live music does add a great touch.

YOU AND YOUR PARTY

A festive atmosphere and good food are the basics of a good party, it's true. Good music and flattering lights help a great deal— But it's *you,* as the hostess or host, who must see that it all goes together. You should have fun at your own party, of course, but you should also be sensitively aware of your guests. Without being oversolicitous, make sure that each person is comfortable, has a drink, and feels he is part of the group.

Don't, however, try to be the life of the party, and don't attempt to entertain everyone. Just introduce each guest upon arrival and help start the conversation with something like: "This is Jane Young; she just returned from Japan." Or: "Jan, you remember Harry Johnson? He is building a new house just a few blocks away from you."

At a large party it is not necessary, or even desirable, to introduce a newcomer to everyone in the room. It stops the conversation, it's a bore, and besides no one can remember "all those names." Instead, find someone you think the new guest will enjoy or take him to a congenial group and bring him into the conversation. Then relax and enjoy yourself. When the surroundings are pleasant and the food is good, it is all but inevitable that people will entertain one another and have a marvelous time.

Index